1981

Eisenhower and the Cold War

Eisenhower and the Cold War

Robert A. Divine

Oxford University Press
Oxford   New York   Toronto   Melbourne
1981

Oxford University Press
Oxford London Glasgow
New York Toronto Melbourne Wellington
Nairobi Dar es Salaam Cape Town
Kuala Lumpur Singapore Jakarta Hong Kong Tokyo
Delhi Bombay Calcutta Madras Karachi

Library of Congress Cataloging in Publication Data

Divine, Robert A
  Eisenhower and the cold war.

  Includes bibliographical references and index.
  1. United States—Foreign relations—1953–1961.
2. Eisenhower, Dwight David, Pres. U.S., 1890–1969.
I. Title.
E835.D54   327.73'0092'4   80–20600
ISBN 0–19–502823–6
ISBN 0–19–502824–4 (pbk.)

First published by Oxford University Press, New York, 1981
First issued as an Oxford University Press paperback, 1981

Printed in the United States of America

To
Barb

Preface

A curious pattern runs through the history of the twentieth-century American presidency. In a period when international affairs have loomed large in national life, we have tended to choose Presidents experienced and skilled only in domestic politics. Rarely do we consider ambassadors or secretaries of state as likely candidates for the White House; instead we turn to governors and senators, men whose credentials are frequently based solely on their handling of problems at home. Yet once in office, we expect these executives to deal with complex foreign situations and to exhibit great skill in diplomacy. Sometimes, as was the case with Woodrow Wilson and Franklin Roosevelt, we are fortunate, and the President proves to be a statesman of the first rank. But sometimes, as with Harry Truman and Lyndon Johnson, the demands of foreign policy outrun his ability, and the result is overreaction and tragedy for the nation and the world.

Dwight D. Eisenhower is the exception to this pattern. Unlike other twentieth-century Presidents, he had little knowledge and experience in domestic affairs, and little aptitude for them, but he possessed a broad background in international matters. As a result, he achieved little at home—no sweeping reforms or significant legislation. Instead, his accomplishments came abroad. For eight years, he kept the United States at peace, adroitly avoiding military involvement in the crises of the 1950s. Six months after taking office, he brought the fighting in Korea to an end; in Indochina, he resisted intense pressure to avoid direct American military intervention; in Suez, he courageously aligned the United States against European imperialism while maintaining a staunch posture toward the Soviet Union. He earnestly sought a reduction in Cold War tensions, traveling twice to European summit meetings, once with modest success and once only to face humiliation and failure due to the U-2 affair. Despite his earnest efforts to achieve a détente with the Soviet Union, by the time he left office in early 1961, crises had sprung up in Berlin, the Congo, Laos, and Cuba that made the Cold War even more intense than it had been when he took over in 1953.

In the pages that follow, I examine the contributions of Dwight Eisenhower to American foreign policy. I write with a basic sympathy for a badly underrated President, yet I am also aware of his shortcomings and his eventual failure to resolve the dilemmas of the Cold War. My purpose is both to demonstrate that, far from being the do-nothing President of legend, Ike was skillful and active in directing American foreign policy, and to try to explain why his efforts for peace and justice frequently failed to succeed in the dangerous world of the 1950s.

I have not attempted to write a full-scale account of Eisenhower's foreign policy. Rather, my approach has been selective. I have concentrated on a number of crucial epi-sodes, ranging from the ending of the Korean War to the U-2 incident, to show the way in which the President played the dominant role in the foreign policy of his ad-ministration. Except for Iran in 1953, I have omitted men-tion of the covert operations conducted by the CIA, not because they are unimportant, but simply because the evi-dence on Eisenhower's role is not yet available. Neither have I explored the recently opened files at the Dwight D. Eisenhower Library in Abilene, Kansas, in any systematic way, a task that would require a long-term research effort. Instead I have relied on the abundant published literature on the Eisenhower administration and on the Cold War crises of the 1950s to support my view of the President. I hope, however, that these essays will stimulate the archival research on which a mature understanding of Eisenhower's place in history must finally rest.

I have incurred many debts. I especially want to express my gratitude to the historians who began the process of reexamining and reevaluating the Eisenhower presidency in the 1970s. Without the pioneering work of Herbert Parmet, Charles Alexander, and Peter Lyon, I could not have written this book. I am equally grateful to the schol-ars who have read portions of the study and offered me their criticisms and comments: Fred I. Greenstein and Richard H. Immerman at Princeton University, John L. Gaddis at Ohio University, and my colleagues at the Uni-versity of Texas, Lewis L. Gould and Michael B. Stoff. I am sure this book would be better if I had followed all of their suggestions. Gerard F. McCauley and Sheldon Meyer encouraged me to undertake this task; Vicky Bijur once again proved to be a very helpful editor. I am grateful to

Margaret Tracy for typing the manuscript. Finally, I wish to thank my wife, Barbara Renick Divine, to whom this book is dedicated. As a converted Democrat, she does not share my appreciation for Eisenhower, but as always she served as my general reader, asking the right questions and insisting on clarity and consistency.

June 1980   R.A.D.
Austin, Texas

Contents

1 / Eisenhower
and the Presidency

There are two ways to view Dwight Eisenhower's path to the White House. The first is to see his selection as President as the almost inevitable result of his role in World War II. After he emerged from the conflict as an authentic national hero, it was only a matter of time before he ended up in the White House. In 1948, when groups within both political parties sought his candidacy, he held back, thus fostering the illusion that he was a modest and unassuming man who could be called to duty only by an extraordinary situation. He thereby avoided the partisan infighting of the Truman years while serving as president of Columbia University. In 1950, Truman brought him again to international prominence by asking him to become the Supreme Commander of the new NATO armed forces in Europe. Then, two years later, when it seemed possible that an allegedly isolationist Robert Taft might win the presidency and lead the nation away from its international responsibilities, Eisenhower proclaimed himself a Republican and agreed to enter the political arena for the first time. After a brief but intense convention fight with Taft, Ike won the GOP nomination and easily defeated Adlai Stevenson in the fall to claim his hero's reward, the presidency of the United States.

The second scenario is less flattering. There are signs that as early as 1943 Eisenhower was aware of his growing stature with the American people and the possibility of reaching the White House someday. Ike's career was not that of the simple soldier following the clear call of duty, but resulted from a deeply held but carefully concealed ambition and from a shrewd manipulation of men and events. George Patton commented in 1943, "Ike wants to be President so badly you can taste it." And biographer Peter Lyon makes a persuasive case for Eisenhower's pursuit of the presidency.[1] He left the Army as soon as possible, after a brief and uncomfortable tour as chief of staff, to take the Columbia presidency, a position which kept him in contact with men of influence yet enabled him to avoid taking firm stands on controversial issues. He accepted the NATO command eagerly, not with a sense of resignation, and he took full advantage of the opportunity to appear again as the savior of Europe, meeting with the heads of state and accepting the plaudits of the people at home and abroad. All the while, he kept in close touch with those working for his political career, even arranging for a young Wall Street banker with excellent GOP connections to serve as a volunteer on his NATO staff. When it appeared that Robert Taft might well win the 1952 Republican nomination, Ike quickly ended his pose of waiting for a draft. The all-out fight for the nomination destroyed any pretense of answering the higher call of duty. In the fall campaign against Stevenson, Eisenhower proved he was an adept and, at times, ruthless politician as he

4

effectively manipulated Richard Nixon, skillfully culti- vated Robert Taft, and appeased Joseph McCarthy by abandoning his wartime mentor, General George Mar- shall. His final elevation could thus be viewed not so much as the product of chance and circumstance as the culmina- tion of a masterfully waged campaign.

The truth probably lies somewhere between these two versions. Eisenhower's entire career suggests the interplay of design and chance. His decision to attend West Point came only after he failed to achieve his first goal of Annapo- lis. During World War I, despite repeated and genuine re- quests for duty overseas, his talent for teaching and organi- zation kept him at home. In the 1920s, he met General Fox Connor purely by accident through George Patton; it was Connor who would arrange for Eisenhower to serve with him in Panama and, in the long lonely hours at that forlorn outpost, supervise an intensive program of reading in both military history and the classics. It was, Ike later admitted, a kind of graduate course that helped him im- measurably in the future. Eisenhower's service as Douglas MacArthur's chief of staff in the 1930s, both in Washing- ton and the Philippines, continued his education in a very different way. MacArthur's awareness of the political as- pect of all military issues added greatly to Eisenhower's understanding of the way the world worked. The two men, so different in their personal styles, parted company in 1939 when Eisenhower left the Philippines after the outbreak of war in Europe.

Ike was fifty years old when he returned to the United States. Although he had learned a great deal from his as- sociation with Connor and MacArthur, he was still only a lt. colonel, having served as a major for sixteen years. At best, he could hope to become a full colonel before retirement. He continued to seek a field command, but once again he was assigned to staff duty, finally ending up under George Marshall an assistant chief of the War Plans Division just after Pearl Harbor. Marshall quickly perceived Ike's talent for military planning and organization and charged him with the task of drawing up the plans for an eventual cross-Channel invasion and writing the directive for the Supreme Commander of the Allied forces in Europe. Then, in June 1942, Marshall chose Eisenhower for this crucial position, reaching down beyond 366 more senior officers to make the appointment.

Eisenhower's subsequent experience in Europe during World War II vindicated Marshall's judgment. He quickly emerged as a master organizer with a special flair for coalition warfare. He realized the importance of establishing a full partnership with the British, impressing on his fellow Americans the need to avoid nationalistic friction, and he insisted on including British officers at all the levels of command. His latent talent for diplomacy enabled him to handle the insistent demands of Winston Churchill and the constant complaints of Charles de Gaulle, and still keep General Marshall and President Roosevelt satisfied that he was not sacrificing American interests in the cause of Allied unity.

In his perceptive study *The Supreme Commander,* Stephen Ambrose comments on the qualities of leadership that Eisenhower had developed by 1943. He had a personal vitality and drive that impressed everyone who came into contact with him. In addition to the famous charm, there was a presence, a sense that Ike had the entire enterprise under control and knew exactly where he was headed. Not an especially large man, he dominated a room when he walked in, and his face, whether breaking into his broad, irresistible grin or reflecting a more somber mood, expressed better than any words his feelings and attitude. He possessed a fiery temper which he kept under control, especially in public, and a penchant for mild profanity. The feeling he projected was one of self-confidence. His mind worked quickly, but he was most at home with practical issues that could be broken down into their components and dealt with systematically. He hated theorizing and left speculation to others. His most effective quality was the sincerity he radiated. His openness and candor dispelled suspicion, and he delighted in winning over potentially hostile individuals. Field Marshal Bernard Montgomery, who had many conflicts with Ike, testified to this quality when he commented, "He has the power of drawing the hearts of men towards him as a magnet attracts the bits of metal. He merely has to smile at you, and you trust him at once."[2]

Eisenhower's greatest gift was his instinctive ability at public relations. Commanding American armies in Europe, he went out of his way to cultivate reporters, aware that they were the eyes through which the nation viewed the war. Harry Butcher, the naval aide and longtime friend who became Ike's wartime public relations expert, testified to his boss's natural ability. Butcher, a prewar vice-president of CBS radio, said that he would get the credit for Ike's performance, credit that he did not deserve because "he is the keenest in dealing with the press I've ever seen, and I have met a lot of them, many of whom are phonies." The general won over the loyalty of the reporters in Europe by appealing to their patriotism. With disarming candor, he would brief them on his plans off the record and treat them as fellow conspirators. As Butcher commented, he "makes them soldiers along with the rest."

Steve Early, FDR's veteran press secretary, attended one of Ike's press conferences near the end of the war and came away a believer. "It was the most magnificent performance of any man at a press conference that I have ever seen," Early commented. "He knows his facts, he speaks freely and frankly, and he has a sense of humor, he has poise, and he has command."[3] While much of the ability was natural, Eisenhower never took the press for granted, and his obvious desire to win over skeptical reporters proved to be both flattering and effective. Later, as President, he would give the press the same careful attention, meeting with them regularly and appointing James Hagerty, the most admired and respected press secretary in recent history, to his White House staff.

Eisenhower's concern for popular approval also indicates one of his most glaring weaknesses, a sensitivity to criticism. In his first major operation, the landings in North Africa in 1942, he authorized the notorious deal with Admiral Jean Darlan to keep the French army from opposing the American and British forces. When this action aroused a storm of criticism in the United States, Eisenhower could not understand why people did not realize he acted only to save lives. In exasperation, he tried to arrange for the flight of his leading detractors to North Africa so that he could confront them personally and convince them of the rightness of his action. Later in the war, when Winston Churchill berated him for rejecting the British proposal for a drive on Berlin and for planning to stop the final offensive into Germany at the Elbe, Eisenhower became very upset. He wrote to Churchill that he was disturbed, and even hurt at the suggestion that he would unduly restrict the activities of the British forces. "Nothing is further from my mind," Ike continued, "and

8

I think my record over two and a half years of commanding Allied forces should eliminate any such idea."[4] Given the dominant role the United States played in the alliance by 1945, there was little Churchill could do, but nevertheless Eisenhower reacted like a hurt child.

This inability to accept criticism was but another side of Eisenhower's desire to be liked by everyone. In the army, with its command system, Eisenhower was protected from adverse comments. But he soon found that political life was different, and he reacted cautiously, always trying to avoid controversial issues that might make him the target of attack. His illustrious reputation, gained so unexpectedly late in life, reinforced his native caution and made him overly protective of his fame. In the White House, instead of using his popularity to advance the interests of his administration, he came more and more to hoard it, placing a higher premium on his adulation by the American people than on any specific achievement.

Despite this flaw, Eisenhower did reveal considerable talent as a political leader during World War II. The deal with Darlan, unfortunate in its ideological implications, still proved essential to victory in North Africa, and Ike took full responsibility for this action. He stood up strongly against Charles de Gaulle, admiring his spirit but resisting his attempts to recapture French glory at American expense. His most serious struggles came with Churchill, who wanted to interfere in almost every aspect of the war and who backed his own generals when they challenged Ike's strategy. With the support of Marshall and Roosevelt, Eisenhower held firmly against the pleas for an invasion of the soft underbelly of Europe and Montgomery's proposed dash to Berlin. At the same time, he was able to retain the respect and admiration of these Allied leaders. As a result, by the war's end he was, as Ambrose notes, "as adept at politics as any professional diplomat."[5]

World War II would serve ever after as Eisenhower's point of reference on world affairs. In common with others of his generation, he viewed appeasement and the Munich conference as the epitome of diplomatic folly. Isolationism was just as bad; "no intelligent man can be an isolationist," he commented to the people of Abilene, Kansas, in June 1945.[6] The United States must remain active in the world, assuming its rightful role of leadership. Despite his service in the Philippines, he was European-centered in his thinking. He shared the Eastern establishment's foreign policy view that American security rested on a stable and friendly Europe, and he had little patience for those Republicans who were oriented toward Asia. Above all, he saw himself as a champion of peace, the soldier who would cap his service to the nation by working for international harmony. Yet even here he had little patience for those who spoke of an ideal world without conflict. Peace, to Eisenhower, was a practical matter. Nations would always have competing interests; the real task was to avoid the resort to armed force. "We must learn in this world," he told John Gunther in 1951, "to accommodate ourselves so that we may live at peace with others whose basic philosophy may be very different."[7]

Eisenhower's outlook on the world grew directly from his personality. Just as he believed that common sense and good will could resolve almost any problem between individuals, he felt that nations could exist in harmony despite their differences. Throughout his career, he had displayed, as Gunther noted, an "instinctive ability to understand the other person's point of view."[8] This empathy, combined with a buoyant optimism, set him at odds with Cold Warriors who believed that the United States was locked in a struggle for survival with the Soviet Union. The clash with the Russians, which he inherited from Truman, was a problem to be managed, not an all-consuming crusade against the forces of evil.

Eisenhower's optimism, his sense of proportion, above all his innate practicality, appealed enormously to the American people. Douglas MacArthur had been an equally successful war leader, but his evident ambition and his theatrical qualities made the voters suspicious. In Eisenhower, a nation beset with the problems of the nuclear arms race and the Red Scare had a man who promised calm leadership and the restoration of national confidence. In the course of the 1952 campaign, he would make the politician's usual promises, but his greatest appeal was his own appearance of serenity. Throughout the war, he had gotten talented men of conflicting views to pull together. He had the knack of delegating authority and yet never surrendering control. He had the ability to stand aloof from the passions of the moment and to assess the broader implications of each situation. In his anecdotal memoir, *At Ease,* he says that after the Chicago Black Sox scandal of 1919, he learned that things were not always the way they seemed. "Behind every human action, the truth may be hidden. . . . Unless circumstances and responsibility demanded an instant judgment, I learned to reserve mine until the last proper moment."[9] What some perceived as excessive caution and even indecision would prove in time to be admirable qualities of patience and prudence that enabled Eisenhower to deal effectively with many of the international crises of the 1950s.

I

The Cold War was at its height in the spring of 1952 when Dwight Eisenhower decided to seek the Republican nomination. The Marshall Plan had helped to put Europe back on its feet economically, but the process of creating an effective NATO defense force had barely gotten started under Eisenhower. There were only a dozen NATO divisions to counter the more than one hundred Soviet formations, and the problem of German rearmament still divided the Western allies. In Asia, the Korean War had settled into a stalemate after the Chinese intervention in late 1950; truce talks that had begun in mid-1951 were stalled over the delicate issue of repatriating unwilling prisoners-of-war. The most ominous development came in the nuclear field, where the Soviets had broken the American atomic monopoly by detonating their first bomb in August 1949. The United States had responded with a crash program to perfect the far more awesome hydrogen bomb, and after a crucial theoretical breakthrough in the spring of 1951, the American H-bomb program was in high gear, with the first test explosion set for the fall of 1952. And the Soviets were only a few months behind in their secret quest for the H-bomb.

Foreign policy posed a difficult political problem for the Republican party. In both the 1944 and 1948 elections, the GOP had chosen not to challenge the Democrats on international affairs, opting instead for a bipartisan position. John Foster Dulles, an experienced international lawyer and diplomat, had advised defeated candidate Thomas Dewey to pursue such a policy, but by the spring of 1952 Dulles had changed his mind. He felt it was vital for the

Republicans to challenge the Democratic policy of containment and to promise the American people a new and bolder stance in world affairs.

In early May, Dulles flew to Paris to confer with Dwight Eisenhower at his NATO headquarters. He brought with him an essay he had written on American foreign policy which would be published three weeks later in *Life* magazine. Warning that containment would lead ultimately to both excessive reliance on military power and to a heavy drain on the American economy, Dulles outlined two new approaches. The first he called retaliation. Instead of investing so heavily in conventional military power to contain the threat of Communist aggression, Dulles suggested a reliance on America's air and nuclear superiority. Without ever mentioning the atomic bomb, he hinted at a willingness to use it as a threat against the Soviet Union. ". . . the free world," he argued, should "develop the will and organize the means to retaliate instantly against open aggression by Red armies, so that, if it occurred anywhere, we could and would strike back where it hurts, by means of our own choosing."[10]

The use of nuclear weapons to neutralize Soviet conventional superiority would enable the United States to implement a new political strategy of liberation. Bemoaning the postwar Russian domination of Eastern Europe, Dulles advocated a moral and spiritual offensive to free these captive nations. The United States should abandon the static policy of containment and instead make it "publicly known that it wants and expects liberation to occur." He did not, however, advocate the use of force. He spoke vaguely about using Radio Free Europe to encourage people to escape from behind the Iron Curtain, and the organization of "task forces" to develop "freedom programs" for each of the captive nations.[11] It might take a decade or more for liberation to occur, but he was confident that in the long run the forces of freedom and democracy would triumph over those of oppression and tyranny.

Eisenhower, who had read earlier drafts of Dulles's essay, was impressed by the concepts of retaliation and liberation. They fitted in with his belief that containment could lead to eventual American bankruptcy. He made no comment about liberation, but he challenged the simplistic notion that all Communist moves could be met with the threat of nuclear war. He wondered how retaliation could be used to counter "Soviet political aggression, as in Czechoslovakia," which "successively chips away exposed portions of the free world." From his experience with NATO, Eisenhower realized the importance of conventional forces "to convey a feeling of confidence to exposed populations, a confidence which will make them sturdier, politically, in their opposition to Communist inroads."[12]

After their meeting in France, Dulles agreed to support Eisenhower's candidacy, but he withheld any public announcement while he strove to hammer out a Republican foreign-policy plank acceptable to both the general and to his main opponent, Senator Robert Taft. The document that finally emerged, after considerable amendment by Taft's supporters, was highly partisan in tone. The Republicans accused the Democrats of abandoning the peoples of Eastern Europe to Communist rule in the "tragic blunders" made at Teheran, Yalta, and Potsdam. A specific repudiation of the Yalta agreement was coupled with a ringing call for the liberation of "captive peoples." Instead of continuing "the negative, futile and immoral policy of 'containment,'" the GOP platform promised to "revive the contagious, liberating influences which are inherent in freedom." Eisenhower accepted this partisan rhetoric, presumably as the price he had to pay for party unity, but he drew the line at the inclusion of the phrase "retaliatory striking power" in the platform. The general felt this meant exclusive reliance on air power and the abandonment of all that he had done to build up NATO. Explaining his opposition to journalist Cyrus Sulzberger, he became red in the face and finally burst out, "I'll be damned if I run on that." Dulles quickly prevailed upon the platform committee to replace the word "retaliatory" with the phrase "force in being, as distinguished from paper plans, of such power as to deter sudden attack," a change Ike found acceptable.[13]

After winning the Republican nomination, Eisenhower seemed willing to embrace the second Dulles slogan, "liberation," in the fall campaign. The promise to take the offensive in the Cold War had great domestic political appeal, especially to ethnic groups such as Polish-Americans who normally voted Democratic. Thus in his first major foreign-policy speech, given at the American Legion convention in late August, Eisenhower declared his opposition to the Soviet tyranny, "a tyranny that has brought thousands, millions of people into slave camps and is attempting to make all humankind its chattel." Without specifying how it would be done, he called upon the American people to join with him in a great moral crusade to liberate the captive peoples. "We must tell the Kremlin," he declared, "that never shall we desist in our aid to every man and woman of those shackled lands who seeks refuge with us." The next day, after a long conference with the candidate, Dulles reaffirmed the liberation concept, telling reporters that what the United States needed to do was to "try to split the satellite states away" from

Russia. "The only way to stop a head-on collision with the Soviet Union is to break it up from within," Dulles concluded.[14]

The Republican liberation rhetoric sent a shudder through Western Europe. Frightened by the prospect of a nuclear war to free the captive nations, Europeans wondered what had happened to the prudent Eisenhower they had known and trusted. At home, the Democrats made the most of their opportunity. Candidate Adlai Stevenson spoke sadly about the risk of a war which would "liberate only broken, silent and empty lands"; President Truman warned bluntly that attempts to liberate enslaved people "might well mean turning these lands into atomic battlefields."[15]

Eisenhower himself was disturbed by the implications of liberation. Upset that Dulles had failed to stress the vital qualification that liberation should be achieved only by peaceful means, the candidate berated him for this omission after a speech in Buffalo in which Dulles talked about air-drops of supplies to anti-Communist freedom fighters. In his next major foreign policy address, the general restated the liberation concept in carefully qualified terms, saying that he intended "to aid by every peaceful means, but only by peaceful means, the right to live in freedom." Then he stressed his devotion to peace by concluding, "The one—the only—way to win World War III is to prevent it."[16]

This speech in Philadelphia on September 4 marks the end of Eisenhower's reliance on liberation in the campaign. He dropped all further references to captive peoples, save for one brief Pulaski Day statement, and he no longer relied on Dulles for drafts of foreign policy speeches. For Eisenhower, the political advantages in liberation were more than outweighed by the implication that he favored a policy that could lead to war with the Soviet Union. His own devotion to peace prevailed.

II

Eisenhower's handling of the Korean War issue showed that he was still willing to exploit foreign policy for political gain. When the war first broke out in June 1950, he staunchly backed Truman's decision to fight, and he stood behind the President when he removed General Mac-Arthur. The stalemate in Korea had made the war increasingly unpopular by 1952, and even though other Republicans sniped at Truman's policy, Eisenhower remained loyal. In his first press conference after declaring his candidacy in June, the general expressed his doubts about launching a major offensive in Korea to achieve victory and then added, "I do not believe that in the present situation there is any clean-cut answer to bringing the Korean War to a successful conclusion."[17]

By the fall, Eisenhower felt differently. Surveys of public opinion and voter sentiment revealed a growing national concern with the stalemated conflict and a belief that Eisenhower could furnish the new leadership needed to end the fighting. The candidate began making references to the war in Korea, defending Truman's decision to fight but questioning his conduct of the war. In early October, he took a new line by suggesting that the administration was wrong in making American youth bear the brunt of battle. "That is a job for Koreans," he said in Illinois. "If there must be a war there, let it be Asians

against Asians, with our support on the side of freedom."
A few days later in San Francisco, Ike stressed the heavy
casualties the United States had suffered in Korea and
then for the first time stated that if elected he would give
"full dedication to the job of finding an intelligent and
honorable way to end the tragic toll. . . ."[18]

Even as Eisenhower was speaking, the dormant war
sprang to life. The Communists broke the lull with a
major offensive on October 6; a week later, General Mark
Clark ordered a counter-strike. For two weeks, American
troops, engaged in bitter, hand-to-hand fighting in the
"Iron Triangle" area, suffered heavy casualties. The Democrats, on the defensive, accused the Republican candidate
of trying to wring votes out of "our ugly, miserable, bloody
ordeal" in Korea.[19] President Truman, angry at Eisenhower's intimation that he knew how to end the conflict,
dared Ike to come forward with his remedy.

Truman's challenge played directly into the hands of
the Republican strategists. Several of Eisenhower's advisers, including speechwriter Emmet Hughes, thought
that Korea was a perfect issue on which to apply the general's reputation as a military expert. Hughes wrote a
speech in which the candidate would promise to go to
Korea if he were elected. He gave it to campaign manager
Sherman Adams, who immediately approved, but they
were afraid that Ike would reject it as too theatrical. When
they showed the text to the general, however, his eyes lit
up, he reached for a pencil, and quickly made a few
changes to sharpen the impact of the key sentence.

Eisenhower made his famous pledge at the height of
the campaign, in a speech in Detroit on October 24. He
singled out Korea as the tragedy that "challenges all men
dedicated to the work of peace." After accusing the Demo-

crats of mishandling the war, he came to his climax. The first task of a new administration, he declared, would be "to bring the Korean war to an early and honorable end." "That job requires a personal trip to Korea," he continued. "I shall make that trip. . . . I shall go to Korea."[20]

"That does it—Ike is in," reporters told Sherman Adams.[21] Nearly all the political commentators agreed that the pledge to go to Korea clinched the election for Eisenhower. He repeated the promise in subsequent speeches, driving home the belief in the minds of voters that the architect of victory in World War II would surely find a way to conclude the limited war in Asia. The beauty of the pledge, however, lay in its very vagueness. All that Eisenhower promised was to make the trip. He left himself complete freedom of action in dealing with the Korean conflict as President. He had thus been able to take political advantage of the Korean War without committing himself in advance to any specific course of action.

III

After Eisenhower's decisive victory at the polls over Adlai Stevenson, most observers assumed that one of his first acts as President-elect would be to appoint John Foster Dulles as secretary of state. Instead, Ike delayed the appointment for several weeks while he canvassed the field. For a time he considered offering the position to John J. McCloy, a leading member of the foreign policy establishment and former American High Commissioner to Germany. Eisenhower finally settled on Dulles, partly out of his respect for his knowledge and experience in foreign policy and partly because Ike knew that the appointment would please the Taft wing of the GOP.

In the course of time, the legend grew that Eisenhower turned over foreign policy completely to his secretary of state, intervening only occasionally to soften the unyielding line that Dulles pursued toward the Soviet Union. Contemporary observers first offered this interpretation, based on the apparent control Dulles exercised over foreign policy, and Sherman Adams confirmed it in his memoirs, the first to appear on the Eisenhower presidency. According to Adams, "Eisenhower gave Dulles a free hand and wide responsibility in shaping the administration's foreign policy." The President was impressed with the fact that Dulles had been active in diplomacy since the Second Hague Peace Conference in 1907, commenting, "Foster has been in training for this job all his life." Aware of Ike's high regard, Dulles, according to Adams, told the President, "With my understanding of the intricate relationships between the peoples of the world and your sensitiveness to the political considerations involved, we will make the most successful team in history."[22]

There is much in the relationship of the two men, however, which does not fit this simple picture. From the outset, Dulles was insecure in his relations with Eisenhower. The President kept him dangling before he appointed him secretary of state, and throughout his presidency, Eisenhower kept a set of independent foreign-policy advisers on hand at the White House. Dulles constantly struggled to prevent men like C. D. Jackson, Nelson Rockefeller, and Harold Stassen from using their White House posts to influence the course of American foreign policy. Adams tells of the frequency of Dulles's visits to the President's office and of the constant telephone calls from the secretary of state, a fact confirmed by the logs kept by the White House staff. In his own memoirs, Ike refers casually to the fact that while traveling abroad, "Secretary Dulles made a constant practice . . . of cabling me a summary of the day's events." After six years, Ike recalled, the cables and other memoranda from Dulles made a stack more than four feet high—hardly an indication of a secretary of state making policy on his own.[23]

In essence, Eisenhower used Dulles. Confident of his own grasp of world affairs, he needed someone who had the knowledge and skill to conduct diplomacy yet would defer to the President. Ike also realized the importance of having a secretary of state who could keep ardent Cold Warriors, especially right-wing Republican senators, happy with administration policy. He knew how helpless Dean Acheson had become, called constantly to testify before congressional committees to justify Truman's policies, which were in fact tough and unyielding toward the Soviet Union. Dulles could serve as the lightning rod, absorbing domestic criticism and warding off attacks from the right with his moralistic rhetoric. On occasion, Ike would complain that "Foster is just too worried about being accused of sounding like Truman and Acheson," but he understood the advantage of having the secretary of state as the target of criticism. ". . . the Democrats love to hit him rather than me," Ike commented to Emmet Hughes. And Ike never had any doubts about who called the shots. ". . . there's only one man I know who has seen *more* of the world and talked with more people and *knows* more than he does," Eisenhower told Hughes, "—and that's me."[24]

The two men formed an effective team. Eisenhower enjoyed the confidence of the American people, and he had a personal relationship with many of the world's leaders. Pragmatic by nature, he was committed to an effort to keep the Cold War manageable, to reduce tensions, and to avoid the dread possibility of a nuclear war. Dulles had a more theoretical cast of mind. Convinced of America's moral superiority, he sought to put the Communists on the defensive. His moralistic and often ponderous public statements gave him the reputation, which he cherished, of being a dedicated crusader against the Soviets; behind the scenes, he proved to have a lucid understanding of the realities of world politics and a surprising gift for the give-and-take of diplomacy. Dulles, the civilian lawyer, had a fondness for the threat of force, while Eisenhower, the military man, preferred the language of peaceful persuasion. The secretary tended to become uneasy in moments of crisis; the President was at his best when the situation became the most tense. One close associate commented about Eisenhower's air of calm relaxation during a critical period: "I realized as never before why a President is so important—to be able to give others, at such a time, an impression of unruffled assurance and confidence." Ike once told Emmet Hughes that "there's just one thing I really *know*. You *can't* decide things in *panic*."[25]

Above all, the two men complemented each other. Ike lacked the stamina and enthusiasm for the daily grind of diplomacy that Dulles took in stride. Though the President was knowledgeable about European issues, he was much weaker on Asia, Latin America, and the Middle East. Dulles helped fill in many of the gaps in Eisenhower's understanding of world affairs. Eisenhower's serene self-confidence helped offset Dulles's personal insecurity. When the secretary fretted about public opinion and the reactions of others, the President could offer him the necessary reassurance, telling him to ignore his critics. And there was no doubt in either man's mind who made the decisions that counted. "The truth is that Dulles did Eisenhower's bidding in matters of high policy," comments presidential biographer Peter Lyon, "and also served as the convenient butt for any criticism of that policy. . . ."[26] Ann Whitman, Eisenhower's private secretary, wrote to a friend after Dulles's death to play down reports of a "new" Eisenhower finally taking command of American foreign policy. "He isn't any different—he has always taken the lead," she wrote. "Perhaps now it is more obvious, but Dulles and the President consulted on every decision and then Dulles went back to the State Department and carried them out."[27]

IV

From the outset of his administration, Eisenhower moved to revitalize the National Security Council and thereby ensure his continuing control over all major foreign policy decisions. The NSC, created in 1947 to coordinate diplomatic and military policy, had never achieved its full potential under President Truman. He had met with the statutory members, who included the secretaries of state and defense, the chairman of the Joint Chiefs, the director of civil defense, and the head of the CIA, infrequently, preferring to arrive at his major decisions independently. Eisenhower asked aide Robert Cutler, a Boston banker, to design a more orderly and systematic procedure, and then in March directed Cutler to put his recommendations into effect under the title, Special Assistant for National Security Affairs. Under the new system, the NSC was broadened to include the secretary of the treasury and the budget director, as well as other officials on an *ad hoc* basis when their expertise was needed. Cutler headed up a Planning Board which prepared a paper on some aspect of national security each week. Cutler circulated the document in advance, briefing the President the day before the NSC met to consider it.

The weekly meetings of the NSC revealed Eisenhower's intense interest and concern for foreign policy. CIA Director Allen Dulles normally opened the sessions with an intelligence briefing, and the Cutler summarized the issue to be discussed. For the next two hours, the members debated the various aspects of the problem before them. Eisenhower followed the discussion closely, trying to stay quiet at first so that others would speak their minds freely, but gradually joining in and expressing his views. The President waited until after the meeting to inform Cutler of the decisions he had reached, and sometimes he called a select few into his office to carry on a further discussion of particularly sensitive topics. Cutler then drew up a Record of Action and supervised its implementation.

Eisenhower liked the new process. He much preferred oral briefings to the reading of long memoranda; in the give-and-take of NSC debate he could weigh the various alternatives and reach carefully reasoned conclusions. He could balance the ideas and suggestions of John Foster Dulles against the views of other advisers. By April, he was telling members of Congress that the NSC had become "the central body in making policy." "Its sessions are long, bitter, and tough," he commented. "Out of that sort of discussion we're trying to hammer policy."[28] Ike attended nearly all the NSC meetings, missing only twenty-nine in eight years, and he was the focal point of the group's discussion. "All remarks were addressed to him," Cutler noted. "When he spoke, everyone listened."[29] Those who attended NSC meetings regularly soon realized that the President, not the secretary of state, was in charge of the administration's foreign policy. "The mythical Eisenhower," commented one NSC member, "who left decision-making to subordinates . . . cannot be found in these records of the most important business he conducted for the nation."[30]

V

In their early months in office, Eisenhower and Dulles had to deal with two issues they had raised in the campaign—liberation and the Korean War. The Republican platform's denunciation of the Yalta agreements and the call for liberation rather than containment led to expectations of a new departure in the administration's policy toward Eastern Europe. In his first State of the Union message to Congress in early February 1953, the President sought to reassure the Republican right. He promised a "new, positive foreign policy" and declared that the United States would not "acquiesce in the enslavement of any people." He would soon ask Congress, he pledged, "to join in an appropriate resolution making clear that this government recognizes no kind of commitment contained in secret understandings of the past with foreign governments which permit this kind of enslavement."

Those who expected an early renunciation of the Yalta agreements were in for a disappointment, however. The President soon realized that repudiation would endanger existing American rights in West Berlin and Vienna as well as run into stiff opposition from the Democrats in Congress. In a press conference in mid-February, Eisenhower commented that he did not feel that it was "feasible or desirable" to deny the entire substance of the Yalta and Potsdam agreements, admitted that he had not found any additional secret agreements, and even defended the secrecy of the wartime accords on military grounds. Concerned about several sweeping "captive nations" resolutions introduced into Congress, Eisenhower and Dulles moved to preempt extreme action by sponsoring a joint resolution that accused the Soviet Union of violating the Yalta agreements "to bring about the subjugation of free peoples."[31]

Democrats, who had maintained all along that it was Soviet violations, not the agreements that Roosevelt and Truman had negotiated, that had led to Communist domination of Eastern Europe, quickly threw their support behind the administration's proposal. The House Foreign Affairs Committee gave its unanimous approval, but in the Senate conservative Republicans, led by Robert Taft, objected. At first they sought an amendment which made it clear that the resolution did not signify a congressional validation of the disputed agreements. When the Democrats refused to accept this reservation, Senator Taft finally permitted the resolution to die in committee after the death of Joseph Stalin in early March. Eisenhower and Dulles, who argued that the change in Russian leadership made it inappropriate to proceed with the captive nations resolution, were relieved to have such a potentially embarrassing and politically divisive issue shelved.

The emptiness of liberation was even more graphically demonstrated in June when rioting broke out in East Berlin and spread to several other cities within the Soviet-occupied zone of Germany. Workers, angered at the imposition of heavier production goals, burned Communist banners on the Unter den Linden and broke open East German jails to free political prisoners. The Soviet Union moved swiftly to restore order; within twenty-four hours the Russian army had brutally crushed the spontaneous uprising. The United States carefully avoided taking any positive action beyond opening food kitchens in West Berlin to feed refugees from East Germany. Eisenhower, who had been aware of the danger of liberation from the outset, kept silent about the Soviet action and refused to let Dulles take any steps that would lead to a confrontation.

VI

The President played a much more active and successful role in redeeming his own personal campaign pledge to end the fighting in Korea. Three weeks after the election, he quietly slipped out of the country for a three-day tour of the fighting front. He conferred briefly with Syngman Rhee, the President of the Republic of Korea, but he spent most of his time visiting American units and talking with the UN commander, General Mark Clark. Clark had prepared a detailed estimate of the forces required for a major offensive to win the war; to his surprise, Eisenhower never asked him what it would take to achieve victory. Instead, the President-elect made it clear that he was more interested in negotiating an honorable peace. In his memoirs, Ike recalled that he quickly concluded that "we could not stand forever on a static front and continue to accept casualties without any visible results. Small attacks on small hills," he decided, "would not end this war."[32]

Over the next few months, Eisenhower considered the alternatives in Korea. Determined not to have the stalemate continue, he examined the possibility of widening the war and launching a general offensive which would include aerial strikes against Manchuria and a blockade of the Chinese coastline. Dulles tended to favor such a course, believing that it was necessary to win in Korea in order to prevent further Chinese advances in Asia. "I don't think we can get much out of a Korean settlement until we have shown—before all Asia—our clear superiority by giving the Chinese one hell of a licking," Dulles told Emmet Hughes.[33] But Eisenhower felt differently. He realized that England and other American allies would oppose an all-out effort in Korea, with the inevitable risk of touching off a world war. "If you go it alone in one place," he told Sherman Adams, "you have to go it alone everywhere. No single nation can live alone in the world."[34]

Another possibility would be to resort to nuclear weapons. General Douglas MacArthur had made this suggestion to Eisenhower shortly after his return from the Korean trip. A solemn warning to the Soviet Union of American intentions to use the atomic bomb would be enough to end the war, MacArthur argued, but he went on to suggest both the "atomic bombing of enemy military concentrations and installations in North Korea and the sowing of fields of suitable radio-active materials . . . to close the major lines of enemy supply. . . ."[35] Eisenhower saw no insurmountable moral problem in the use of atomic weapons, but he shared the doubts of the Joint Chiefs of Staff about the effectiveness of tactical bombs on the deeply entrenched Communist forces in Korea. He also realized the rift this would open up with our allies, and he worried about a possible Soviet response against the defenseless cities of Japan.

The President finally chose a variant of MacArthur's proposal. Instead of publicly warning the Soviet Union that we planned to use nuclear weapons to end the Korean conflict, Eisenhower decided to let the Chinese, Russians, and North Koreans know that the United States was prepared to "move decisively without inhibition in our use of weapons" unless there was satisfactory progress in the peace talks. "In India and in the Formosa Straits area, and at the truce negotiations at Panmunjom," Eisenhower recalled, "we dropped the word, discreetly, of our intention. We felt quite sure it would reach Soviet and Chinese Communist ears."[36]

Stalin's death may have been as influential as the veiled threat of nuclear force. In late March, the Chinese suddenly responded favorably to an earlier American request for an exchange of sick and wounded prisoners-of-war. More significantly, the Communists also indicated a willingness to renew negotiations, suspended since the fall of 1952, on the key issue—American refusal to permit forced repatriation of prisoners-of-war. A large proportion of the more than 100,000 North Korean and Chinese captives did not want to return to their homelands. China had rejected an earlier Indian proposal for a neutral repatriation commission to decide the fate of those unwilling to go home, but in the talks that resumed in Panmunjom on April 6, the Communist representatives accepted voluntary repatriation in principle. Presumably either direct pressure from the Soviet Union or Chinese uncertainty of Russian support for a hard line after the death of Stalin had led to this sudden change in Communist policy.

When the truce talks reached an impasse in mid-May, Eisenhower decided it was time to step up the pressure. In the course of a two-day visit to India, Secretary Dulles informed Prime Minister Nehru that the United States might feel compelled "to use atomic weapons if a truce could not be arranged."[37] Eisenhower and Dulles were sure that Nehru would pass along this warning to Peking. At the same time, the President sent new orders to General Mark Clark in Korea authorizing him to break off the truce talks if the Chinese rejected the final American offer. If the fighting resumed, Clark commented in his memoirs, "then I was to prosecute the war along lines we had not yet taken to make the Communists wish they had accepted our terms."[38] Finally, the administration transferred atomic warheads to American bases in Okinawa.

The Chinese responded in early June by accepting the American formula for the repatriation of prisoners-of-war. A last-minute attempt by Syngman Rhee to sabotage the truce negotiations by releasing 25,000 Communist prisoners held in South Korea delayed the final negotiations, but on July 27, 1953, UN and Communist representatives signed eighteen copies of the armistice agreement at Panmunjom. Syngman Rhee expressed his displeasure by boycotting the ceremony, and several Republican senators criticized the Eisenhower administration for failing to achieve a unified Korea. The American people, however, were relieved that a long and unpopular war had finally come to an end. The President struck the appropriate note of caution in his message to the nation on the truce: "we have won an armistice on a single battleground, not peace in the world."[39]

It was still an impressive achievement. Six months after taking office, Eisenhower had fulfilled his implicit campaign promise and ended the divisive Asian conflict. He quite properly had given it priority in the early months of his administration, and he clearly was the architect of the successful strategy. Stalin's death helped by adding a new element of uncertainty in the Communist ranks and thus inclining China toward a peaceful solution. The President had steered a careful course between Dulles's urging of a military victory and MacArthur's call for a public nuclear challenge. Several years later, Dulles would try to claim the credit by telling a reporter that he had gone to the brink of war to achieve the Korean settlement and thus stirred up a controversy over "brinksmanship." But it was Eisenhower, in his own characteristically quiet and effective way, who had used the threat of American nuclear power to compel China to end its intervention in the Korean conflict. Perhaps the best testimony to the shrewdness of the President's policy is the impossibility of telling even now whether or not he was bluffing.

2 / Massive Retaliation and Asia

The end of the Korean War marked only the beginning of Eisenhower's involvement with Asian issues. Throughout his years in the White House, he wrestled with difficult and thorny problems arising from the Communist victory in China and the spread of revolutionary nationalism in the Far East. Eisenhower, whose knowledge and experience were centered in Europe, felt ill at ease dealing with Asia and thus relied heavily on John Foster Dulles in handling these crises of the 1950s. Both men were blinded by the prevailing belief that monolithic communism lay behind the turmoil in the Orient, rather than a variety of nationalist aspirations, and this misconception doomed American policy.

Eisenhower's first priority on taking office was to reassess American strategy in the Cold War. The lesson of the Korean War seemed clear to the new President—neither the American people nor the American economy could stand a succession of limited, conventional wars. The public resented the commitment of American troops to battle for anything less than complete victory; the heavy deficits such conflicts incurred would slowly sap the nation's resources. On board the *U.S.S. Helena,* on his way back from the pre-inauguration trip to Korea, Ike made clear his determination to solve "the great equation" of maintaining a strong national defense at a bearable cost to the nation.

Two participants in the discussions on board the *Helena* outlined possible solutions. The first, Admiral Arthur Radford, commander-in-chief of the Pacific fleet, pointed out that it was costly and inefficient to have American forces scattered around the world. Radford argued for a new policy of concentration, reducing American garrisons abroad and building up a mobile, strategic reserve in the United States to be used to reinforce our allies in case of a Communist attack. This suggestion led the second participant, John Foster Dulles, to renew the proposal for retaliation that he had made to Eisenhower in Paris nearly a year before. To avoid the expense of manning the perimeter around the Communist sphere with conventional forces, Dulles advocated primary reliance on American nuclear striking power as a deterrent against any Soviet-sponsored aggression. Eisenhower did not reach any firm conclusions on board the *Helena,* but by making clear his conviction that "the relationship . . . between military and economic strength is intimate and indivisible," he indicated his receptivity to the ideas of Radford and Dulles.[1]

The search for a new military stance in the Cold War led to Operation Solarium, named for the White House sun room where it was conceived in May 1953. The President appointed separate task forces to examine three broad options available to the United States. The first was containment, the policy inherited from the Truman administration, with its stress on both allies abroad and the readiness of the United States to join with them in fighting conventional wars like the one in Korea to stem Communist aggression. A second alternative to be studied was essentially an amalgam of the Dulles-Radford proposal. The United States would draw a line about the world and warn the Soviet Union that any penetration could lead to a nuclear response. The third group was to examine the campaign slogan of liberation to see if the new administration should conduct a program of economic, psychological, and possibly even para-military warfare against the Communist bloc.

The three task forces worked through the summer at the Naval War College and then submitted their recommendations to the National Security Council. By October, the NSC had ruled out the alternative of liberation and had decided to continue the policy of containment with modifications to permit a greater reliance on nuclear retaliation to hold the line against Communist expansion in Third World areas.

At the same time, Eisenhower was seeking ways to cut back the heavy defense budget he had inherited. In May, he replaced the Joint Chiefs of Staff with four new appointees, including Admiral Radford as chairman. In a White House meeting, he instructed them to make a complete survey of the nation's strategic requirements and to take into consideration diplomatic and fiscal factors as well as narrowly military ones. Despite this injunction, the recommendations they made disappointed the President and his chief economizer, Secretary of the Treasury George Humphrey. Balancing reductions made possible by the end of the Korean War against new expenditures occasioned by the Soviet Union's successful test of the hydrogen bomb in August, the Chiefs urged a continuation of both existing force levels and defense spending at approximately $35 billion a year.

In explaining and defending this recommendation, Admiral Radford pointed out that the Chiefs had to plan for every possible contingency, ranging from limited war to general conventional war on up to all-out nuclear war. If, however, the military were to be authorized to rule out conventional warfare and to plan on using nuclear weapons whenever it was technically advantageous to do so, then they could achieve significant reductions in manpower and large cuts in the total defense budget. Despite opposition from Army Chief of Staff Matthew Ridgway, Radford's suggestion proved attractive to both Eisenhower and Humphrey. The secretary of the treasury later said that he was convinced that it was American nuclear striking power that "kept peace in the world. And all the rest of these soldiers and sailors and submarines and everything else," he continued, "comparatively speaking, you could drop in the ocean, and it wouldn't make too much difference."[2]

Eisenhower accepted the new strategy, and it was incorporated into his administration's statement of basic national security policy, NSC 162/2, adopted on October 30, 1953. After a statement outlining the nature of the Soviet threat to American well-being, NSC 162/2 stipulated the necessity for the United States to maintain "a strong military posture, with emphasis on the capability of inflicting massive retaliatory damage by offensive striking power." Near the end of this review of national strategy, the document stated specifically that "in the event of hostilities, the United States will consider nuclear weapons to be as available for use as other munitions." While in fact the President still retained the ultimate decision on the use of nuclear weapons, his assent to NSC 162/2 amounted at least to a promise to the Joint Chiefs that he would authorize nuclear retaliation in case of overt Communist aggression.[3]

The reliance on strategic power enabled the Eisenhower administration to make a significant reduction in both force levels and defense spending. The "New Look," as it was quickly dubbed, called for cutting back the Army from its post–Korean War strength of twenty divisions to a 1957 goal of fourteen, a drop of nearly half a million men. The Navy was to undergo much less shrinkage, losing only a handful of combat ships and slightly more than 100,000 sailors, while the Air Force would increase from 115 to 137 wings and add 30,000 men. In essence, the new strategy called for implementing Radford's idea of reducing American forces overseas and relying instead on the ground forces of allies backed by a mobile reserve based in the United States. Planning included the possible use of tactical atomic weapons in local wars, while the chief reliance was placed on massive American retaliatory power designed to deter the enemy from acts of aggression. Thus in Asia, the plan called for the complete withdrawal of American combat troops from Korea and a readiness to use strategic weapons against the aggressor's centers of power. The result would be "more bang for the buck," relying on the Air Force to act as the primary deterrent against Communist attack, while reducing the defense budget from $35 to $31 billion a year.

Although John Foster Dulles did not participate in the formation of the "New Look," he found the strategy congenial and became the first administration spokesman to reveal its full implications to the American people. In a speech to the Council on Foreign Relations in New York on January 12, 1954, the secretary of state announced that as a result of a "basic decision" of the National Security Council, the United States no longer would depend on local defensive forces but instead would rely on "massive retaliatory power" to halt aggression. The advantages, Dulles explained, would be to deprive the enemy of the freedom to "pick the time, place, and method of warfare." The Joint Chiefs no longer had to plan to meet every Communist probe with conventional forces; they could now "depend primarily upon a great capacity to retaliate, instantly, by means and at places of our choosing."[4]

Dulles's speech set off a great furor. Critics charged him with reckless language, labeling his policy "massive retaliation" and warning that the Soviet Union might well decide that the threat of nuclear war was so incredible that it would encourage rather than prevent aggression. Eisenhower characteristically refused to join in the ensuing debate, telling reporters that the secretary "was merely stating what, to my mind, is a fundamental truth" and adding, "I think no amplification of the statement is either necessary or wise." But Eisenhower had in fact read and approved the text of the speech in advance and had apparently penned in the key sentence warning of a "great capacity to retaliate, instantly, by means and at places of our own choosing."[5] The policy reflected Eisenhower's belief that it was necessary to regain the initiative in the Cold War. Instead of waiting for the Communists to probe along the perimeter for weaknesses, Ike preferred to warn them of America's determination to respond, possibly with nuclear weapons. The policy was deliberately ambiguous, designed to make the enemy weigh the danger of a limited challenge turning into a nuclear holocaust. In essence, Eisenhower had opted for a policy of deterrence to replace containment—the threat of force as a way to avoid limited wars and unlimited defense expenditures. The President made clear his confidence in massive retaliation at a press conference on March 17, 1954, when he explained that the heart of the strategy lay in the uncertainty it engendered in the enemy. The beauty of the policy, Ike commented, was that no one "would undertake to say exactly what we would do under all that variety of circumstances."[6]

I

Massive retaliation met its first test in Indochina in 1954. A civil war had been in progress since the late 1940s in which the Vietminh, the Communist-dominated insurgents led by Ho Chi Minh, were gradually gaining the upper hand over the French. The United States had repeatedly urged the French to grant independence to the Associated States of Vietnam, Laos, and Cambodia, but France had extended only limited self-rule under Emperor Bao Dai. In May 1950 the Truman administration had made a firm commitment to assist the French in Indochina, and by 1953 the United States was bearing a large share of the cost of the civil war. When Eisenhower became President, he placed an even higher value on the French effort in Indochina. A National Security Council recommendation on August 5, 1953, stated that the "loss of Indo-China would be critical to the security of the U.S." and warned that "any negotiated settlement would mean the eventual loss to Communism not only of Indo-China but of the whole of Southeast Asia."[7]

The French responded by adopting the Navarre Plan, named for their new commander in Indochina, General Henri Navarre, which called for raising 100,000 additional Vietnamese troops and reinforcing them with nine battalions of French soldiers. General Navarre would then use this combined force of 550,000 men to launch a new offensive against the Vietminh in the Red River Delta. Despite misgivings expressed privately by both Eisenhower and the Joint Chiefs of Staff, the United States gave its approval and a new commitment of $385 million in military aid. The Navarre Plan, Dulles announced in late 1953, would "break the organized body of Communist aggression by the end of the 1955 fighting campaign." Navarre was less optimistic; he told his superiors in Paris that the best he could achieve would be a stalemate that would permit a negotiated peace with the Vietminh.[8]

The situation became critical in early 1954 when General Navarre decided to force a showdown by holding on to a remote outpost deep in the interior of Vietnam near the border of Laos and China. Dien Bien Phu was a major road center but not a natural fortress. Located in a deep valley, it became the site of a protracted seige, as the Vietminh, with Chinese Communist support that had intensified after the end of the Korean War, began to close in on the 12,000 French defenders. As the French position deteriorated, the government in Paris sent Chief of Staff Paul Ely to Washington to seek additional American support. In conversations with Admiral Arthur Radford, chairman of the Joint Chiefs, Ely sketched a bleak picture. To his surprise, Radford began to outline a possible American response, an air strike against the Vietminh at Dien Bien Phu that had been drawn up by both American and French officers in Saigon. Operation Vulture, as the project was named, would involve 60 American B-29s from bases in the Philippines, supported by 150 American carrier-based fighters. In one massive thrust, American air power, possibly including tactical atomic bombs, would devastate the besieging Communist forces and rescue the French from certain defeat.[9]

While Ely returned to Paris to inform his government of Radford's proposal, the Eisenhower administration searched for a solution to the French dilemma in Indochina. Vulture was Radford's own idea and did not even have the support of other members of the Joint Chiefs. President Eisenhower had been agonizing for months over the plight of Indochina and had arrived at four basic assumptions that would guide his policy through the ensuing crisis.

The starting point of the President's policy was his firm belief that Indochina was vital to the security of the United States. The area was important for many reasons. It was rich in raw materials like tin and rubber; its geographical location placed it at the crossroads of Southeast Asia; its millions of people deserved to live in freedom, not Communist domination. But above all else, the fall of Indochina to Communism, he believed, would lead to the loss of all Southeast Asia. Citing the famous comparison to a row of falling dominoes in a press conference on April 7, 1954, Ike warned that Burma, Thailand, and Indonesia would quickly follow the loss of Indochina to Communism and that, in turn, would endanger "the so-called island defensive chain of Japan, Formosa, of the Philippines and to the southward; it moves on to threaten Australia and New Zealand." "So," he concluded, "the possible consequences of the loss are just incalculable to the free world." Two weeks later, he changed the metaphor, but not the sense of peril, when he likened Indochina to "a sort of cork in the bottle, the bottle being the great area that includes Indonesia, Burma, Thailand, all of the surrounding areas of Asia with its hundreds of millions of people, and its geographical location that controls lines of communications, to say nothing of the great products of the region, some of which we must have."[10]

Despite the importance of this region, the French, Eisenhower's second assumption argued, had proved irresponsible. Instead of meeting the legitimate desire of the Vietnamese for independence and self-government, they had refused to give a firm pledge to end their colonial rule. The government of Joseph Laniel, Ike complained, hinted at independence "in an obscure and round-about fashion—instead of boldly, forthrightly and repeatedly." Eisenhower had urged the French to adopt this stand when he served as NATO commander in 1951, and he reiterated the advice in a letter to his successor, General Alfred Gruenther, in 1954. The French, he wrote, must "unequivocally pledge independence to the Associated States upon the achievement of military victory." The only way to win in Indochina, Ike concluded, was with the full participation of "local Asiatic peoples." The French had also failed to conduct the war effectively. Eisenhower had been appalled at Navarre's decision to place his forces at Dien Bien Phu and had tried to warn the French of the likely result. "You *cannot* do this!" Ike recalled telling a French diplomat, adding that the French were surely "smart enough to know the outcome of becoming emplaced and then besieged in an exposed position with poor means of supply and reinforcements." "Never before," the President concluded, "had I been so sad to be so right."[11]

The third assumption was the necessity of securing the

support of our allies in any effort to save Indochina from Communist domination. Eisenhower remembered how useful it was in the Korean War to have the support of the United Nations, and he was convinced that cooperative action with Britain, Australia, New Zealand, and some of the independent nations of Southeast Asia was essential to reassure world opinion and to avoid the appearance of "a brutal example of imperialism." As he explained to General Gruenther, "no Western power can go to Asia militarily, except as one of a concert of powers."[12] The French, he feared, only wanted to find a face-saving way to cut their losses; in February they had agreed to a Russian proposal for a five-power conference, dealing with both Indochina and Korea, to convene in Geneva in late April and to include Communist China. The United States had agreed reluctantly, fearful that the French would be ready to negotiate away their position in Indochina. Thus last-minute American intervention to rescue France would not solve the underlying problem, how to preserve Indochina, and eventually all Southeast Asia, from Communist domination.

Secretary of State Dulles finally came up with the solution that Eisenhower was looking for. In a speech to the Overseas Press Club of America on March 29, a speech that Eisenhower had gone over line by line in advance, Dulles reiterated the administration's belief in the strategic significance of Indochina, pointing out that it sits "astride the most direct and best developed sea and air routes between the Pacific and South Asia." Its loss would mean "a grave threat to the whole free community," and therefore the Eisenhower administration was calling for "united action" on the part of the entire free world to save this vital region from Communist control. Although

Dulles never defined what "united action" meant, the new slogan summed up the key feature of Eisenhower's approach to the Indochina crisis—the insistence that any action the United States took be a cooperative one with our allies.[13]

The President's final assumption was that Congress must grant prior authorization for any steps that he took in Southeast Asia. Remembering the criticism that his own party leveled at Truman for neglecting congressional approval for the Korean War, Eisenhower insisted upon proceeding along constitutional lines. In a press conference in February, Eisenhower defended a decision to send air force ground crews into Indochina temporarily and then added, "No one could be more bitterly opposed to ever getting the United States involved in a hot war in that region than I am." A month later, when a reporter asked if the presence of American mechanics in Indochina might not lead to war, the President said unequivocally that America was not going to become involved unless Congress exercised its constitutional right to declare war. In his memoirs, Ike was even more outspoken. "Part of my fundamental concept of the Presidency is that we have a constitutional government," he wrote, "and only when there is a sudden, unforeseen emergency should the President put us into war without congressional action."[14]

II

The Indochina crisis reached its first climax in early April. On Saturday, April 3, Secretary Dulles and Admiral Radford met with eight congressional leaders to seek their support for a resolution authorizing American military intervention in Indochina. Radford outlined the essentials of Operation Vulture, but under questioning he admitted that American ground forces might be needed if the bombing did not succeed and that the other members of the Joint Chiefs had not approved of the proposed air strike to relieve Dien Bien Phu. The congressional leaders voiced their reservations about involving the United States in another Asian land war so soon after Korea, and they finally indicated that they would only approve of intervention if the Eisenhower administration could secure the firm support of the NATO allies, particularly Great Britain.

The next evening, Dulles and Radford met with the President at the White House. The secretary reported on the reaction of the legislative leaders which ruled out any immediate attempt to bail out the French. The President, who agreed fully with the congressional view, then laid down three conditions for American intervention in Southeast Asia. First, France and the Associated States of Indochina must request American military participation; second, Britain, Australia, and New Zealand must agree to take part; and finally Congress must first give its consent. The second condition was the most crucial, since it was the key to congressional support. Therefore, Eisenhower sent a cable to British Prime Minister Winston Churchill in which he outlined the need for "united action" to save Indochina from communism and asked the British to confer with Dulles on ways to achieve this goal. In somber terms, the President warned Churchill that the situation "could be disastrous" and appealed to his sense of history by reminding him that "we failed to halt Hirohito, Mussolini and Hitler by not acting in unity and in time."[15]

While Eisenhower and Dulles were perfecting their

plans for "united action," the French cabinet listened to General Ely's report on his trip to Washington and decided to ask the United States to implement Vulture as the only way to avoid defeat at Dien Bien Phu. At one in the morning on April 5, Ambassador Douglas Dillon cabled Dulles that both Premier Laniel and Foreign Minister Georges Bidault were "now asking for US carrier aircraft support at Dien Bien Phu." The secretary promptly cabled back a negative response, pointing out that American intervention would have to be based on a "full political understanding with France and other countries" and on prior congressional approval. "After conference at highest level," Dulles concluded, "I must confirm this position." The President was even blunter, chewing out Admiral Radford on April 5 for misleading the French and telling him that Vulture was "politically impossible."[16] Eisenhower and Dulles had no intention of rescuing the French at the eleventh hour at Dien Bien Phu, only to see them then negotiate a compromise settlement on Indochina at the forthcoming Geneva conference. Instead, they were intent on working out a broad plan to save all Southeast Asia from Communist domination.

"United action" eventually met the same fate as Vulture. Dulles conferred with British Foreign Secretary Anthony Eden in London, but the two men failed to agree on what to do. The British favored a negotiated settlement of Indochina and preferred to delay any consideration of military intervention until after the Geneva Conference. The French proved equally intractable. They wanted help at Dien Bien Phu, but they strongly opposed the internationalization of the Indochina war, which they still considered an internal French concern. A second French request for an air strike to relieve Dien Bien Phu in late April met with a cool reception in Washington. Eisenhower condemned the French for using "weasel words in promising independence" to the Vietnamese, and he refused to consider going into Indochina "as junior partners" while France retained "authority in that region."[17] Dulles tried once more to secure British cooperation, probably in an effort to escape having the blame for the eventual fall of Dien Bien Phu placed solely on the United States, and again the British firmly refused to become involved.

The surrender of the French garrison on May 8 brought one last American proposal for military action. In a meeting that day with Dulles and National Security Advisor Robert Cutler, Eisenhower indicated that he was willing to sound out the French once more on possible American intervention in cooperation with Australia and New Zealand, but not Britain. The conditions that the President laid down, however, virtually precluded French acceptance. In addition to a firm promise of independence for the Associated States, France would have to agree to permit the United States to train the Vietnamese forces, "share responsibility for military planning" with the United States, and pledge to "stay in the fight" and not negotiate away Indochina at Geneva. Eisenhower asked Dulles to draw up a resolution authorizing American intervention, but he never had the opportunity to present it to Congress. The French backed away, indicating that all they wanted was one American marine division in Indochina and refusing again to make the unequivocal grant of independence for the Associated States. The refusal of Australia and New Zealand to act independently of Britain ruled out cooperative action, and even the Joint Chiefs expressed reluctance to intervene at this late date. On May 26, the military leaders sent a memorandum to the secretary of defense urging that any American intervention be limited to "air and naval support directed from outside Indochina." In the judgment of the Joint Chiefs, *"Indochina is devoid of decisive military objectives and the allocation of more than token* U.S. armed forces *in Indochina would be a serious diversion* of limited U.S. capabilities."[18]

This final American decision not to become militarily involved in Indochina raised the question of how close the United States actually came to intervention in 1954. At the time, the prospects seemed very real. "There is considerable fear among the Americans," wrote New York *Times* foreign correspondent Cyrus Sulzberger from Paris on April 24, "that we are hovering on the verge of World War III." When Vice President Nixon's off-the-record statement on April 16 that "the Administration must face up to the situation and dispatch forces" leaked, there was a genuine war scare in the United States. Strong congressional opposition, including a warning by Senator John F. Kennedy that a war in Indochina would be "dangerously futile and self-destructive" and an emotional outcry from Senator Lyndon Johnson against "sending American GI's into the mud and muck of Indochina on a bloodletting spree," indicated that the nation was far from ready for direct military involvement.[19]

No one understood this political reality better than Dwight Eisenhower. In his memoirs, he reports that he told his advisers as early as January 1954 that "I could not at that moment see the value of putting United States ground forces in Southeast Asia." The events of March and April did not change his thinking. He told congressional leaders on April 26 that, while he favored united action in Indochina in concert with our allies, they must "realize that our effective role does not lie in furnishing ground troops." Eisenhower got full support for this view from Army Chief of Staff Matthew Ridgway, who warned that intervention in Indochina would lead to casualties as heavy as those America endured in the Korean War. The policy of massive retaliation had already reduced American ground forces, Ridgway argued, and intervention in Indochina would dangerously weaken American commitments to the defense of Europe. In a sober estimate, he calculated that seven U.S. divisions "would be required to win a victory in Indochina" and as many as twelve if the French withdrew and the Communist Chinese intervened. He passed on this report to Eisenhower, and later commented in his memoirs. "To a man of his military experience, its implications were immediately clear."[20]

There still remained the possibility of limited intervention, such as the air strike that Admiral Radford had proposed in Vulture. General Nathan Twining, the air force chief of staff, later regretted that the United States had not dropped "three small tactical A-bombs" around Dien Bien Phu. The result would have been to "clean those Commies out of there and the band could play the 'Marseillaise' and the French would come marching out of Dien Bien Phu in fine shape." Eisenhower was briefly tempted. On April 1, he remarked casually that he would like to order a "single strike, if it were almost certain this would produce decisive results." "Of course," he added, "if we did, we'd have to deny it forever." But upon reflection the President decided against this form of military adventure. The use of air power alone, he wrote later, "would comprise an act of war and would also entail the risk of having intervened and lost." "I had no intention," he continued, "of using United States forces in any limited action when the force employed would probably not be decisively effective." He considered the idea of an air strike to relieve Dien Bien Phu "just silly." "After those people are deployed, and secreted all around in the jungle," he asked, "how are we, in a few air strikes, to defeat them?" He told Walter Cronkite in a television interview in 1961 that "I couldn't think of anything probably less effective . . . unless you were willing to use weapons that could have destroyed the jungles all around the area for miles and that would have probably destroyed Dien Bien Phu itself, and that would have been that."[21]

Eisenhower received strong support from his advisers in rejecting the air power solution. Admiral A. C. Davis, a Pentagon planner, warned that the United States "should not be self-duped into believing the possibility of partial involvement—such as Naval and Air units only. One cannot go over Niagara Falls in a barrel only slightly." General Ridgway made the same point in his evaluation of the risks involved in intervention. He stated that "air and naval forces alone" would not be decisive, and he claimed that even the use of atomic weapons would not "reduce the number of ground forces required to achieve a military victory in Indochina."[22] The President accepted the advice of Davis and Ridgway, and wisely rejected the more daring proposals of Radford and Twining.

There was, however, one form of force that the President was prepared to employ, the threat of nuclear weapons to deter Chinese intervention in Indochina. Recalling the Korean experience, the President told his aides in late April that while it would be foolish to drain our resources and strength in a land war in Indochina, the participation of China would demand an American response. In that case, he said, "we could scarcely avoid . . . considering the necessity of striking directly at the head instead of the tail of the snake, Red China itself." Secretary of State Dulles delivered this warning to Peking in early June when he declared that Chinese involvement in Indochina "would be a deliberate threat to the United States itself," and thus "we could not escape ultimate responsibility for decisions closely touching our own security and self-defense." The *Pentagon Papers* reveal that Eisenhower and Dulles were not bluffing. On May 26, the President approved recommendations by the Joint Chiefs that called for "employing atomic weapons, whenever advantageous . . . against those military targets in China, Hainan and other Communist-held offshore islands" in case of Chinese intervention in Indochina. The President made clear, however, that such action could be taken only after Congress had granted permission and in cooperation with our European allies. "Unilateral action by the United States in cases of this kind would destroy us," Ike told Robert Cutler. "If we intervened alone in this case we would be expected to intervene alone in other parts of the world."[23]

III

The outcome of the Indochina crisis reflected the logic of massive retaliation. Eisenhower, determined not to become involved in another Korea, shrewdly vetoed American military intervention, either with ground forces or by a limited air strike. At the same time, however, he permitted Dulles to warn the Chinese not to expand the conflict and attempt to spread their control throughout Southeast Asia. The warning apparently had some effect at the Geneva Conference. After the fall of the Laniel government in early June, Pierre Mendès-France became Premier and pledged to end the fighting in Indochina within thirty days. Despite the favorable Communist military position, both Russia and China put pressure on Ho Chi Minh to accept the division of Vietnam at the 17th parallel, with the promise of elections to determine the political future of all Vietnam in 1956. With considerable reluctance, the Vietminh accepted this compromise, and the fighting ended in mid-July.

The United States did not sign the Geneva accords. Instead the American representative, Walter Bedell Smith, simply took note of the arrangements and promised not to "disturb them" by the "threat or the use of force."[24] Some portions of the accords were unpalatable, especially the ban on introducing new forces and military equipment and the prohibition on either portion of Vietnam entering into a military alliance. But both Eisenhower and Dulles were relieved that the election for national unification was postponed until 1956. (Ike was sure Ho Chi Minh would win "possibly 80 per cent" of the vote if it were held in 1954.)[25] They saw an opportunity to build up a strong anti-Communist government in the South and to make it the barrier to further Communist inroads into Southeast Asia. With France humiliated, the United States could now emerge as the protector of South Vietnam.

Dulles outlined the new American policy in Indochina to a group of congressional leaders in late June. Claiming that the United States would be able to "salvage something" from the Indochina debacle, Dulles spoke optimistically of becoming "free of the taint of French colonialism." Now the United States could draw a line against Communism and "hold this area and fight subversion within it with all the strength we have." Eisenhower was in full agreement with this approach. He supported the appointment of Ngo Dinh Diem, a fiercely anti-Communist Vietnamese who had spent several years in exile in the United States, as the new Premier of South Vietnam under Emperor Bao Dai. He saw in the new regime in Saigon the best hope for the future. "We must work with these people," Ike told Jim Hagerty, "and then they themselves will soon find out that we are their friends and that they can't live without us."[26]

The key to the new policy was for the United States to take the place of a defeated France in Southeast Asia. In a memorandum to the secretary of defense on August 4, the Joint Chiefs of Staff stressed the need for American support for a "strong, stable civil government" in South Vietnam and called for the complete "withdrawal of French forces, French officials and French advisers from Indochina." The National Security Council agreed with this analysis, and on August 20, 1954, President Eisenhower approved a new threefold American policy in Southeast Asia. It called for military aid to South Vietnam in which the United States would "work with the French only so far as necessary to build up indigenous forces able to provide internal security." Economically, American funds would no longer flow to Indochina through the French but instead go directly to Diem, thereby cutting off France from "the levers of command." Finally, the United States would support Diem politically and encourage him to broaden his government along more democratic lines.[27] Thus the Eisenhower administration resolved the Indochina crisis by writing off North Vietnam and by replacing France as the principal protector of Southeast Asia against Communist expansion.

Dulles completed the new Asian policy in September

when he arranged for the creation of the Southeast Asia Treaty Organization (SEATO) in Manila. The new alliance was designed to parallel NATO, but it was only a pale imitation. The United States, Great Britain, France, Australia, and New Zealand joined with Thailand, the Philippines, and Pakistan to prevent the "extension of Communism." The absence of such influential Asian nations as India, Indonesia, and Burma made SEATO suspect from the outset, as did the failure to include any automatic provisions for collective action against aggression. The treaty simply stated that each member would "meet the common danger in accordance with its constitutional process."[28] Nor did the new alignment include Laos, Cambodia, and South Vietnam, since these states were forbidden under the Geneva accords from entering into any military alliance. Dulles attempted to remedy this weakness by including a protocol that extended SEATO protection to the area of Indochina.

SEATO and the new American commitment to South Vietnam marked the administration's attempt to salvage whatever it could from what the National Security Council termed the "disaster" in Indochina. Eisenhower had already set firm limits to American military intervention in Southeast Asia, telling congressional leaders that it would be a "tragic error to go in alone as a partner of France." Dulles had responded by seeking "united action," but the British refusal to act prior to the Geneva Conference had blocked this plan. The formation of SEATO and the decision to replace France in South Vietnam were as far as Eisenhower would go in 1954. The President can be criticized for committing the United States to the regime of Ngo Dinh Diem, but at least he had stood firmly against direct American involvement. Townsend Hoopes was right when he praised "the solid common sense of a President with a feeling in his bones that military adventures ought not be undertaken without allies, and that decisions involving war and peace must have explicit congressional participation and support."[29]

IV

On the morning of September 3, 1954, Communist batteries on the mainland of China began lobbing artillery shells into the Chinese Nationalist positions on the island of Quemoy. Two American soldiers died in the opening onslaught of what proved to be the severest test yet of the administration's policy of massive retaliation.

Quemoy and its sister island, Little Quemoy, were part of a large number of offshore islands that had remained in the hands of Chiang Kai-shek's forces after their expulsion from China in 1949. The two Quemoys lay directly across from the port city of Amoy. To the north, the nineteen islands of the Matsu chain controlled access to Foochow, while still further north the Nationalists occupied the Tachen islands. All told, there were 75,000 troops on the offshore islands, with 50,000 concentrated on Quemoy. Chiang used them to harass the Communists with commando raids against the China coast and attacks on Communist shipping. For the Nationalists on Taiwan, separated from the mainland by the 100-mile wide Taiwan Strait, Quemoy and Matsu were potential stepping stones for an ultimate return to China. The islands were equally important to Peking. The Communists resented the Nationalist presence on their very doorstep (it was like having a foreign power on Staten Island, some sympathetic Americans pointed out), and they needed to control Quemoy and Matsu before they could launch their long promised conquest of Taiwan.

American policy toward the offshore islands was in flux at the time of the Chinese bombardment. President Truman had ordered the Seventh Fleet into the Formosa Strait in 1950 to prevent an invasion of Taiwan during the Korean War, but Republicans had claimed the American naval presence inhibited a Nationalist return to the mainland, and so Eisenhower had announced in 1953 that the fleet would no longer restrain Chiang Kai-shek. When Communist Foreign Minister Chou En-lai renewed the pledge to conquer Taiwan in August 1954 and warned the United States to keep its hands off, Eisenhower responded by telling reporters that "any invasion of Formosa would have to run over the Seventh Fleet." But Quemoy and Matsu were a different matter. Unlike Taiwan, they had always been under Chinese control and were virtually a part of the coastline. ". . . were we to intervene in the offshore islands," warned Walter Lippmann, "we would be acting on Chinese territory in a Chinese civil war."[30]

Eisenhower was vacationing in the Colorado Rockies when the crisis developed in early September; Dulles was in Manila presiding over the birth of SEATO. In Washington, the Joint Chiefs of Staff voted three-to-one on September 6 to recommend that the President authorize Chiang to bomb mainland China and if this provoked an assault on Quemoy, to permit American forces to join in the island's defense. General Ridgway dissented, warning that such action would mean full-scale war with China. The President agreed with Ridgway and immediately sent Dulles to Taiwan to restrain Chiang Kai-shek. Then on

September 12, Eisenhower convened the National Security Council at Lowry Air Force Base near Denver for its first meeting ever outside Washington. Admiral Radford, backed by air force chief of staff Nathan Twining and chief of naval operations Robert B. Carney, made the case for defending the offshore islands. While he admitted Quemoy and Matsu were not vital to the defense of Taiwan, Radford maintained that the loss of these islands would have "bad, possibly disastrous, psychological effects" on the Chinese Nationalists. Eisenhower disagreed strongly with this reasoning. "We're not talking now about a limited, brush-fire war," the President shot back. "We're talking about going to the threshold of World War III. . . . Moreover, if we get into a general war, the logical enemy will be Russia, not China, and we'll have to strike there." Dulles, who had originally supported the Joint Chiefs' recommendation, now backed away from the use of force, and suggested instead that he explore the possibility of a UN ceasefire. The meeting ended on that anticlimactic note, with one relieved official saying, "the President personally saved the situation."[31]

Intermittent Chinese shelling of Quemoy continued for the next several months while Dulles sought a solution to what he termed "a horrible dilemma." When Chiang blocked an approach to the UN, Dulles concentrated on completing the negotiation of a bilateral defense treaty with the Chinese Nationalists. The text of the treaty spelled out clearly the American commitment to defend Formosa, but the fate of the offshore islands was left hanging. Eisenhower deleted an attempt by Dulles to include them specifically, and finally the President agreed only to extend the American commitment to "such other territories as may be determined by mutual agreement." In addi-

EISENHOWER AND THE COLD WAR

tion, Eisenhower insisted on placing new restraints on Chiang to prevent him from embroiling the United States in any Nationalist attempt to invade the mainland. Thus on December 10, Dulles exchanged letters with the Nationalist ambassador stipulating that the "use of force" from any area controlled by Chiang "will be a matter of joint agreement."[32]

The defense treaty represents Eisenhower's attempt to regain control of a very slippery situation. Having rebuffed the military's desire for intervention, he needed to placate the strong pro-Chiang and anti-Communist factions within his own party. In November, Senator William Knowland of California, the Republican minority leader whom critics dubbed the "Senator from Formosa," had demanded that the administration blockade the coast of China. Ike had ignored this request, telling Knowland that the United States had "to have the courage to be patient." By signing a treaty to defend Formosa, Ike was giving the GOP right wing its minimum demand. At the same time, by insisting on restraining Chiang Kai-shek, the President protected himself against the danger of automatic involvement in one of the generalissimo's military adventures. Once again Eisenhower had displayed "skilled manipulation of an extremely ambiguous diplomatic and domestic political situation."[33]

V

The crisis in the Taiwan Straits reached a new peak in mid-January 1955 when the Communists began an attack on the Tachen islands, some two hundred miles northwest of Formosa. Although these islands were not vital to the defense of Taiwan, Eisenhower decided it was time "to draw the line" against further Chinese aggression. In a series of meetings with his national security advisers, the President decided to assist the Nationalists in evacuating the Tachens while strengthening the defenses of Quemoy and Matsu. At the same time, Eisenhower announced that he would ask Congress for a joint resolution authorizing the use of force to protect Formosa and the nearby Pescadores. In his message to Congress, Ike made clear his desire to defend Formosa, and then asked the legislators to grant him authority to include "closely related localities" in the American commitment. The President was deliberately ambiguous about the offshore islands; he wanted to keep the Chinese guessing whether or not the United States in fact would resist an attack on Quemoy and Matsu.[34]

Eisenhower's middle course immediately stirred up controversy. Although the House quickly passed the desired resolution by a vote of 410 to 3, in the Senate Herbert Lehman introduced an amendment to limit the resolution to Formosa and the nearby Pescadores and specifically to exclude Quemoy and Matsu. At the same time, Admiral Carney objected to Ike's order to evacuate the Tachens, urging instead that the United States help the Nationalists defend these islands. The President overruled his naval adviser, and in February American ships helped the Nationalists withdraw from the Tachens. The opposition in the Senate quickly dissolved after press secretary James Hagerty released a statement in the President's name stipulating that American forces would be used "purely for defensive purposes" on the basis of a presidential decision "which he would take and the responsibility for which he has not delegated." Somewhat later Eisenhower explained to House Speaker Sam Rayburn that he would not commit

American troops to defend Quemoy and Matsu unless he was convinced that a Chinese attack on them was part of a larger assault on Formosa itself. He had not "made that decision" and would not make it until he knew "the circumstances surrounding any given attack." On that basis, the Senate rejected the Lehman amendment, 74 to 13, and then passed the Formosa resolution by the overwhelming vote of 83 to 3.[35]

While stressing the conditional nature of the American commitment to defend the offshore islands, the President made a much more specific pledge to Chiang Kai-shek in a private letter on January 31 in order to secure his agreement to evacuate the Tachens. It was apparently this secret pledge that Eisenhower was referring to in a February letter to Winston Churchill, who favored abandoning the offshore islands to the Communists. "The morale of the Chinese Nationalists is important to us, so for the moment, and under existing conditions, we feel they must have certain assurances with respect to the offshore islands," Ike explained. He hastened to add that he was not obligated to respond automatically to an attack on Quemoy and Matsu—he would make a distinction "between an attack that has *only* as its objective the capture of an off-shore island and one that is primarily a preliminary movement to an all-out attack on Formosa." When Churchill responded that the offshore islands were not essential to the defense of Formosa—the Seventh Fleet could easily "drown any Chinese would-be invaders of Formosa"—Ike replied with a variation of the domino thesis. "The French are gone—making it clearer than ever that we cannot afford the loss of Chiang unless all of us are to get completely out of that corner of the globe," Eisenhower wrote. "This is unthinkable to us. . . ."[36]

The Formosa Straits crisis had, in fact, presented Eisenhower with an almost impossible situation. In September, he had instinctively resisted the military's demands to defend Quemoy and Matsu. But in his attempts to placate Chiang and the China bloc in Congress, he had come dangerously close to committing the United States to defend the offshore islands against any Chinese attack. The distinction between an assault aimed only at the islands and one that included Formosa was, as Eisenhower confessed, "a difficult one." As long as the Nationalists held Quemoy and Matsu, it would be impossible for the Communists to launch an invasion of Taiwan, but it did not necessarily follow that the seizure of the islands was part of a broader plan to capture Formosa. The best Eisenhower could do was to keep the mainland Chinese guessing by repeatedly stating that the American response to an attack on the islands "would have to depend on circumstances as they might arise." Thus, as he told Rayburn, "Foster and I are living twenty-four hours a day with the question of what to do if something happens in Quemoy and Matsu. This is the most difficult problem I have had to face since I took office."[37]

VI

The climax came in March 1955. Returning from a two-week trip to Asia, Secretary of State Dulles told the President on March 10 that the situation in the Formosa Strait was "far more serious" than he had realized. The Communists were bent on conquering Formosa as well as the offshore islands, Dulles reported. "If we defend Quemoy and Matsu," he continued, "we'll have to use atomic weapons." Ike immediately sent an aide to Pearl Harbor to confer with the commander of the Pacific Fleet, and his report was equally pessimistic, predicting a Chinese attack on the islands in late March.[38]

While Eisenhower mulled over this estimate, Dulles went public with his threat of atomic reprisals. In a statement on March 12, the secretary spoke of "new and powerful weapons of precision which can utterly destroy military targets without endangering unrelated civilian centers." Puzzled by such an assertion of a "clean" nuclear strike, one of Dulles's aides checked with the CIA and came back with the estimate that tactical nuclear strikes at Chinese airfields and troop concentrations opposite Quemoy and Matsu would kill between 12 and 14 million Chinese civilians! Despite this report, Dulles told the press on March 15 that the administration was prepared to use tactical atomic weapons in case of war in the Formosa Straits. The next day, a reporter asked Ike to comment, and the President replied affirmatively. "Now, in any combat where these things [tactical atomic weapons] can be used on strictly military targets and for strictly military purposes," Eisenhower declared, "I see no reason why they shouldn't be used just exactly as you would use a bullet or anything else." This was not an off-the-cuff response by the President, who prepared carefully for his press conferences. He made the nuclear threat after careful consideration. "I hoped this answer," he wrote in his memoirs, "would have some effect in persuading the Chinese Communists of the strength of our determination."[39]

The result was a war scare at home. Eager hawks rallied to Eisenhower's side. "Either we can defend the United States in the Formosan Straits—now, or we can defend it later in San Francisco Bay," declared Senator Alexander Wiley of Wisconsin. General James Van Fleet, the former commander of the Eighth Army in Korea, wanted the administration to send American troops to Quemoy and Matsu and then if the Communists continued shelling the islands, Eisenhower could "shoot back with atomic weapons and annihilate the Red effort." Admiral Carney escalated the sense of crisis when newspapers leaked his off-the-record comments in late March predicting a Chinese attack on Matsu by mid-April and began speculating about an American preemptive nuclear strike. Democrats made the most of the ensuing fanfare. Herbert Lehman led a Senate effort to revive his earlier amendment to exclude Quemoy and Matsu from the American commitment to defend Formosa, while Majority Leader Lyndon Johnson warned against undertaking "an irresponsible adventure for which we have not calculated the risks." Adlai Stevenson expressed "the gravest misgivings about risking a third world war in defense of these little islands," a remark that infuriated Eisenhower, as did a columnist's charge that "all our Allies, except Generalissimo Chiang Kai-shek, regard this as the wrong war, at the wrong time, and at the wrong place."[40]

Eisenhower moved to quiet the fears at home that his nuclear warning to China had raised. When Jim Hagerty advised him to duck any questions at his March 23 press conference on the sensitive Formosa Straits issue, Ike replied, "Don't worry Jim . . . I'll just confuse them." The President then proceeded to tell the reporter who asked him if he planned to use nuclear weapons to defend Quemoy and Matsu that he could not answer directly, but that nothing in warfare was predictable, and that "every war is going to astonish you in the way it occurred, and in the way it is carried out." A week later, Eisenhower arranged for Hagerty to inform journalists that "the President did not believe war was upon us." Privately, Eisenhower was voicing the same sentiment in a diary note. ". . . I believe hostilities are not so imminent as is indicated by the forebodings of a number of my associates," he wrote. "I have so often been through these periods of strain that I have become accustomed to the fact that most of the calamities that we anticipate really never occur."[41]

Eisenhower was right. Despite the risk he took in stimulating concern at home, his nuclear threat apparently got through to Peking. On April 23, Foreign Minister Chou En-lai, in Bandung, Indonesia, for a meeting of Third World nations, spoke of Chinese friendship for the American people, said that they "do not want to have a war with the United States of America" and suggested negotiations to "discuss the question of relaxing tension in the Far East and especially the question of relaxing tension in the Taiwan area." The State Department immediately dismissed this proposal out of hand, treating it as purely a propaganda move by China to impress nonaligned nations. But Eisenhower took it seriously, and four days later expressed a willingness to open negotiations "if there seemed to be an opportunity for us to further the easing of tensions." On August 1, 1955, discussions got under way in Geneva between American and Chinese diplomats. Although the Geneva talks failed to resolve the issues of the offshore islands and the fate of Formosa, they provided a face-saving way for China to stop its shelling of Quemoy and thus to end the crisis.[42]

Ever since, most commentators have been critical of Dulles and Eisenhower for taking the nation to the brink of war over the remote offshore islands. The prevailing view is to condemn Dulles for practicing "brinksmanship" and to praise Eisenhower for showing restraint. Thus Townsend Hoopes placed Dulles "in full command of day-to-day operations" at the height of the crisis in March and had Eisenhower taking "a rare initiative in the realm of his Secretary of State" in April to save the situation. Peter Lyon is closer to the truth when he points out that Eisenhower was in complete control throughout and that "the foreign policy of the United States, so widely attributed to Dulles, bore the stamp of Dwight Eisenhower, and it was not a rubber stamp." But Lyon is unduly critical of Eisenhower's role in the Formosa Straits crisis, and he credits Chou En-lai for displaying the "self-possession, maturity, willingness to conciliate, friendliness and an easy, relaxed self-confidence" that permitted a peaceful settlement.[43]

In reality, Eisenhower not only determined American policy throughout the crisis, but carried it out to a successful conclusion. He took Dulles's concept of massive retaliation and refined it. Instead of relying on the certainty of nuclear retaliation to frighten America's opponents, as his critics complained, Ike preferred to keep the Communists guessing. He introduced a note of deliberate ambiguity into American policy. He refused to announce publicly whether or not he would commit the United States to oppose an attack on Quemoy and Matsu, and thereby kept the Chinese Communists off balance. When the crisis became most serious, he used a measured nuclear threat to warn the Chinese without insulting them or provoking them into an attack. The beauty of Eisenhower's policy is that to this day no one can be sure whether or not he would have responded militarily to an invasion of the off-shore islands, and whether he would have used nuclear weapons. Critics who seize on his statement to Hagerty, "Don't worry, Jim . . . I'll just confuse them," to belittle Ike fail to understand this strategy of deliberate deception. What he wanted to do above all else in the Formosa Straits crisis was to maintain his freedom of action and to keep control over a complex series of events. It is a tribute to his leadership that he was able, as he finally allowed himself to boast in his memoirs, to thread his way "with watchfulness and determination, through narrow and dangerous waters between appeasement and global war."[44]

VII

A renewed crisis in the Formosa Straits forced Eisenhower to invoke massive retaliation one last time in Asia. In many ways the situation was similar to 1955. The Chinese Communists began shelling Quemoy on August 23, 1958, with the Peking radio broadcasting threats to "smash the American paper tiger and liberate Taiwan." Chiang Kai-shek had helped provoke the attack by a massive troop buildup on Quemoy, contrary to American advice, and by conducting commando raids on the China coast. The United States faced the old dilemma of how to distinguish between an attack on the offshore islands and one directed against Taiwan—a situation further complicated by the fact that 100,000 Nationalist soldiers, one third of Chiang's entire army, were stationed on Quemoy.

There were also important differences. The Soviet Union, as Eisenhower noted in his memoirs, now possessed a formidable nuclear striking force which included the H-bomb; the threat of American strategic retaliation now involved far more serious risks. The Chinese resort to a naval blockade of Quemoy complicated the tactical situation—could the United States threaten atomic reprisal against this form of harrassment? And finally, Chiang Kai-shek posed an even more serious problem than he had in 1955. A firm statement of American willingness to defend Quemoy and Matsu might well encourage him to carry out his repeated boasts to return in force to the mainland.[45]

Eisenhower decided that the wisest course of action was to do what he had done in 1955—"keep the Communists guessing." Dulles preferred a firm statement of American intentions, but he followed Ike's wishes and released a letter to the chairman of the House Foreign Affairs Committee in which he stated that it would be "hazardous" for anyone to assume that the administration's response to an attack on the offshore islands "could be considered or held to a 'limited operation.'" This veiled threat of a nuclear response reflected Eisenhower's determination to retain control of a fluid situation. When Chiang Kai-shek pleaded with Ike for a "categorical statement" of American intentions and for the delegation of authority to commit American forces to the local commander, the President refused to do so. As he explained in his memoirs, "I insisted that I would assess developments as they occurred. Therefore, I kept to myself the decision to employ U.S. forces."[46]

Eisenhower did, however, try to reassure Chiang by having Dulles release a public statement after the two men conferred at Newport, Rhode Island—the summer White House—on September 4. Dulles brought a memo to this meeting in which he spelled out the dire consequences that would follow the loss of the offshore islands—the fall of Taiwan itself and the Communist seizure of all Asia—and recommended the use of small atomic bombs ("air bursts, so that there would be no appreciable fallout or large civilian casualties"). Although Eisenhower approved this private formulation of policy, he authorized Dulles to release a much more circumspect public statement which repeated the traditional formula linking the defense of the offshore islands to an attack on Formosa. Noting the repeated Chinese threat to conquer Formosa, Dulles did add that "we have recognized that the securing and protecting of Quemoy and Matsu have increasingly become related to the defense of Taiwan." In a background press briefing that same day, Dulles, identified only as a "high official," went much further and made an unequivocal pledge to defend Quemoy.[47]

This new effort at brinksmanship only deepened the crisis. Informed of the American willingness to employ "small air bursts without fallout," British Prime Minister Harold Macmillan expressed fear that the Russians would "join in" and the world would be "on the brink of World War Three." On September 7, Soviet leader Nikita Khrushchev sent a candid warning to Eisenhower: "An attack on the Chinese People's Republic is an attack on the Soviet Union." In the United States, Democratic spokesmen such as Adlai Stevenson and John F. Kennedy criticized Eisenhower and Dulles for risking war over Quemoy, and State Department mail ran 4-to-1 against the administration's policy. The President moved to calm the nation in a televised address on September 11. He reiterated his commitment to defend Formosa and to stand firmly against aggression as a matter of principle. But then he expressed his desire to enter into negotiations and closed with a prediction, "I believe that there is not going to be any war."[48]

The crisis, in fact, was already past. On September 6,

Chou En-lai had offered to resume the bilateral ambassadorial talks with the United States that had begun in Geneva in 1955 and had been broken off in July 1958 after their transfer to Warsaw. Although the new talks proved no more successful than those in 1955 in resolving the underlying issues in the Formosa Straits, their resumption signaled Chinese understanding that the United States would defend the offshore islands and thus ended the likelihood of a direct Communist attack. For the next few weeks, however, the Communists tried to starve the Nationalists out of Quemoy by intensifying their shelling and naval blockade. Eisenhower ordered a reinforced Seventh Fleet to help Chiang supply his troops on Quemoy, although American ships were ordered not to cross the traditional three-mile limit. By October, the blockade was broken. The mainland Chinese suspended the shelling for a brief period, and then bewildered the world by announcing a policy of bombarding Quemoy every other day, thus permitting supplies to resume while displaying formal objection to the continued Nationalist presence. As Eisenhower commented on this peculiar end to the crisis, "I wondered if we were in a Gilbert and Sullivan war."[49]

The second Formosa Straits crisis thus proved to be briefer but more intense than the first. The risk of escalation, as Macmillan had feared, was much greater, though probably exaggerated. In his memoirs, Ike stated that, had he been "forced to intervene to save the offshore islands," he would have acted to "restrict our air strikes to shipping and to the nearby Communist airfields. We would not launch an immediate attack on the interior of China as a 'punishing' operation," he continued. The President was more specific in his reassurance to the worried British. On

69

September 21, he told Foreign Secretary Selwyn Lloyd that he was "against the use of even tactical atomic weapons in a limited operation."[50]

Some commentators, notably Townsend Hoopes, argued that Dulles maneuvered Eisenhower into a needlessly reckless position in 1958. The evidence, however, indicates that the President was in control of the situation throughout. He resisted pressures from both Dulles and Chiang to take an unequivocal stand to defend the offshore islands, preferring the ambiguity that served him so well in 1955. Even the Dulles background commitment of September 4 furthered Ike's ends; it helped persuade the Chinese to seek a peaceful settlement and yet enabled the President to take a more conciliatory position in his September 11 address to the nation. Once he had persuaded the Communist Chinese that it was too hazardous to attack Quemoy, he then used more limited naval power to relieve the besieged garrison and end the blockade. "I was determined that by every possible means we should avoid expanding hostilities more than absolutely necessary," Ike explained in his memoirs.[51] The fact that he did so demonstrates once again the flexible nature of his policy of massive retaliation.

3 | Eisenhower
and the Middle East

The unstable Middle East presented President Eisenhower with an even greater challenge than Asia in the 1950s. When the General took office in 1953, the Cold War had not yet flared up in this strategic area where Europe, Asia, and Africa come together. A number of factors, however, made the outlook grim. England and France, the European nations which had dominated the Middle East in the past, were no longer able to exercise their former authority. The French had retreated from Syria and Lebanon after World War II and were approaching a dangerous civil war in Algeria; the British faced a new nationalist regime in Egypt that was demanding the end of imperial control and the eventual take-over of the Suez Canal, long considered the lifeline of the British Empire. The emergence of an independent Israel in 1948 and its subsequent victory against its Arab neighbors had led only to greater tensions in the area. The United States backed the Jewish state, but at the same time tried to block an arms race in the Middle East by joining with England and France in

1950 in issuing a Tripartite Declaration which warned against "the use of force" by either the Jews or the Arabs and promised to "take action" if they found any nation "preparing to violate frontiers or armistice lines."[1]

Oil posed the most serious questions of all. In the 1940s, American petroleum companies had become active in the Middle East, once the almost exclusive preserve of British, French, and Dutch corporations. Mobil and Exxon had a stake in Iraq, Gulf in the newly developing fields in Kuwait, and four American companies—Standard of California, Texaco, Mobil, and Exxon—became partners in Aramco (American Arabian Oil Company) in 1948 to exploit the virtually untapped reserves in Saudi Arabia. The American firms reaped huge profits from the cheap crude in the Middle East, most of which was refined and sold in Western Europe. Domestic production still met the needs of the American market, but by the early 1950s the NATO allies were heavily dependent on Middle Eastern supplies for both their armed forces and their internal energy needs. Any move by the Soviet Union into the Middle East would threaten not only the Suez route to Asia but the source of the economic vitality of a booming Western Europe, an area deemed vital to American security.[2]

The complications that oil posed for American diplomacy were compounded by a deliberate policy of allowing private companies to conduct their activities with a minimum of government supervision or interference. The Truman administration began this abdication of responsibility in 1950, when the State Department arranged for a change in the form of royalty payments to King Ibn Saud. Instead of a fixed sum on each barrel of oil, Aramco would split the profits of its operations with Saudi Arabia fifty-fifty, with the payment listed as a tax paid to a foreign government. The Truman administration then permitted the four companies that owned Aramco to deduct this foreign payment as a business expense in calculating their American income taxes. By this ingenious "golden gimmick," King Ibn Saud received nearly $50 million in the first year, while the American treasury lost the same amount. The advantage for the State Department, however, was to provide a secret subsidy for Saudi Arabia, and later for other Arab states, while officially the United States still stood before the world as the prime supporter of Israel. Instead of going to Congress for foreign aid appropriations, where the pro-Israel lobby might prove a difficult obstacle, the State Department permitted the oil companies to become "the paymasters of the Arab states," and thus avoided "a clash between its two conflicting foreign policies."[3]

Eisenhower, inheriting this reliance on American oil companies, continued and even extended the practice in the Iranian crisis of 1953. The problem had first arisen in 1951 when an ardent Iranian nationalist, Dr. Mohammed Mossadeq, had become Prime Minister and had nationalized the oil fields and refineries formerly owned by the Anglo-Iranian Oil Company. Mossadeq was a deceptive leader. To many he seemed comical, a figure of ridicule who appeared in public wearing pajamas and wept openly about his country's ills. Some saw him as a dupe for the Communists (despite the fact that he opposed the Tudeh, the Iranian Communist party); others, like British Foreign Secretary Anthony Eden, viewed him as symbolizing "an elemental nationalism." Actually, he came from a wealthy, landowning family and was a shrewd politician who exploited the nationalist grievances that all Iranians felt to-

ward the British.[4] The English government considered
and rejected the use of force (influenced partly by American opposition), and then settled for a boycott, pulling out
all its technicians and experts from the oil fields and from
the great Abadan refinery in October 1951. For the next
two years, the brotherhood of oil, led by the seven great
international corporations that dominated the distribution
process, shut Iranian oil off from the world market, creating a serious economic crunch in Iran. American firms
cooperated gladly with Anglo-Iranian; the great boost in
production in Kuwait and Saudi Arabia to make up the
Iranian deficit created huge profits for Exxon, Gulf, Mobil, Texaco, and California Standard.

President Eisenhower, however, saw the situation as
potentially dangerous. Although he did not share the British distaste for Mossadeq, he worried that the continued
crisis might provide Russia with the opportunity to move
into Iran. When Eden visited Washington in March 1953,
the new President warned him that "the consequences of
an extension of Russian control of Iran, which he regarded
as a distinct possibility, would either involve the loss of
the Middle East oil supplies or the threat of another world
war." According to Eden, Eisenhower "seemed obsessed by
the fear of a Communist Iran," and the foreign secretary
finally gained American agreement that they should begin
to look for "alternatives to Mossadeq."[5]

Meanwhile, the Iranian leader appealed to President
Eisenhower. In a message sent on May 28, 1953, Mossadeq
described the financial hardship caused by the international oil boycott and then asked for American help, either
in the form of oil purchases or outright economic assistance. Near the end, Mossadeq hinted that he might be
forced to turn to Russia, telling Eisenhower that there

could be "serious consequences, from an international viewpoint as well, if this situation is permitted to continue." Eisenhower took more than a month to reply, and when he did, he coldly rebuffed Mossadeq. The American people, he explained, would resent extending aid to Iran when all that was required to settle the problem was "a reasonable agreement" with the British. Then Ike gave his own warning, which proved prophetic. "I note the concern reflected in your letter at the present dangerous situation in Iran," he stated, "and sincerely hope that before it is too late, the Government of Iran will take such steps as are in its power to prevent a further deterioration of that situation."[6]

Mossadeq chose to ignore Ike's subtle hint. In July, he dissolved the Iranian parliament, received a Soviet aid mission, and began to accept support from the Tudeh party. At that point, Eisenhower authorized the CIA to organize and carry out a political coup. Kermit Roosevelt, a grandson of President Theodore Roosevelt who had mastered the craft of intelligence in World War II with the OSS, arrived in Teheran in early August and made the necessary preparations. He contacted General Fazlollah Zahedi, who agreed to take over from Mossadeq with the approval of the Shah, and then he arranged for the cooperation of key elements in the Iranian army and imperial police and recruited a mob, consisting of weightlifters and gymnasts as well as army and police NCOs dressed in civilian clothes, to take to the streets. An abortive attempt to place Zahedi in power forced the Shah, then merely a figurehead, to flee to Rome, where he conferred with CIA Director Allen Dulles. Then three days later Roosevelt orchestrated what one CIA colleague called "a real James Bond operation" and what Eisenhower later described as

75

"more like a dime novel than an historical fact." Mossadeq went to prison for three years, Zahedi took office as Prime Minister, several hundred Iranians lost their lives, and the Shah emerged as the real ruler of Iran. Privately, the President praised Kermit Roosevelt for acting "intelligently, courageously, and tirelessly," even awarding him the National Security Medal in secrecy; publicly, Eisenhower cabled his congratulations to both General Zahedi and the Shah and on September 5 formally committed $45 million in economic aid to the new Iranian government.[7]

Ike was pleased with the outcome in Iran. He confided in his diary on October 8 that with American assistance the negotiations between Britain and the new Iranian government should quickly resolve the oil issue and thus "give a serious defeat to Russia intentions and plans in that area." There was never any question in the President's mind that security in the Cold War was the vital issue in Iran, but he also recognized the important role that petroleum played. He worried about the effect of the long boycott on the Iranian economy and the difficulty the Shah and General Zahedi might face in marketing Iranian oil in the face of world overproduction of crude on the order of 1 million barrels a day. But with his usual optimism, the President concluded "this is a problem that we should be able to help solve."[8]

Herbert Hoover, Jr., son of the former President, was Eisenhower's chosen instrument. Appointed special petroleum adviser to Secretary of State Dulles, Hoover, an experienced oilman who had earlier advised the Iranian government, flew to Teheran and began to act as middleman between the British and the Iranians. Hoover quickly realized that the Shah could not simply restore the British monopoly; one possible way out would be for American companies to share in the new oil arrangements in Iran. The five major American companies involved in international oil all were reluctant to participate. They had benefited from increased production elsewhere in the Middle East as a result of the Iranian shutdown and already produced more crude than they needed for the current market. But called upon by Hoover to serve the national interest by moving into Iran, they finally agreed, in return for a promise that their concerted action would be exempt from American anti-trust laws. President Eisenhower thereupon sent Attorney General Herbert Brownell a note quoting a National Security Council memorandum adopted early in 1953 that stated that "the enforcement of the Antitrust laws of the United States against the Western oil companies operating in the Near East may be deemed secondary to the national security interest. . . ." With this assurance, the five American members of the "seven sisters" who effectively controlled the distribution of nearly all the world's oil agreed to participate in the consortium that Hoover now put together.[9]

The negotiations took nearly a year, but in October 1954 the Iranian parliament approved the final terms. Iran would retain ownership of the oil fields and refineries once held by Anglo-Iranian; a consortium of eight Western companies would buy and distribute the Iranian oil, dividing the profits equally with the government of Iran. Anglo-Iranian received compensation in payments from both Iran and its seven new business partners. Anglo-Iranian received a 40 per cent interest in the new consortium, the five American companies 40 per cent (8 per cent each), Royal Dutch Shell was given a 14 per cent share, and a French company the remaining 5 per cent. (A year later eight American independents were added to the arrangement, their combined 5 per cent share coming from the 40 per cent of the five American majors.) The Shah had proved to be a tough negotiator, benefiting from the precedents and policies of Mossadeq, but the Western companies outwitted him by agreeing among themselves to a complicated and secret formula to limit Iranian production each year and thus to serve their own global oil interests at the expense of Iran. As one oil man later commented about the reluctant participation of the American companies in the Iranian consortium, "This was most profitable patriotism."[10]

President Eisenhower always viewed his role in resolving the Iranian crisis favorably, listing it among the positive accomplishments of his administration. The important issue for the President was not the additional profits for American corporations, but the containment of the Soviet Union and the preservation of Western Europe's vital oil supplies. He genuinely believed that Russia was poised to enter Iran in 1953 and that only the CIA had prevented a Communist victory. As for the oil, the President was much more concerned with its strategic significance for the NATO allies in Europe than for any American economic benefit. Several years later he agreed with adviser Dillon Anderson that "an adequate supply of oil to Western Europe ranks almost equal in priority with an adequate supply for ourselves." ". . . the West must, for self-preservation," Eisenhower concluded, "retain access to Mid-East Oil."[11] Nevertheless, the President, by permitting the continuation of a policy which relied on private American corporations to conduct the nation's oil diplomacy in the Middle East, surrendered power that belonged in the White House and State Department to the directors of five American companies whose ultimate loyalty was to their stockholders, not the American people. Moreover, by using the CIA to overthrow the legitimately constituted government and install the Shah in power, Eisenhower sowed the seeds of future trouble in Iran. In this case, a short-term triumph led to a long-term defeat for the United States.

I

The Egyptian seizure of the Suez Canal on July 26, 1956, presented Eisenhower with the most severe crisis of his entire presidency. For the next four months, as the 1956 election campaign ran its course, the President attempted to restrain England and France, and when these efforts failed, he applied economic and political pressure to secure a peaceful resolution of the Suez crisis. In the process, the Western alliance suffered severe strains, but Eisenhower achieved his major goals—preventing a global war and blocking Soviet domination of the vital Middle East.

The events leading to the Suez crisis revealed a growing American determination to supplant the English as the major Western influence in the Middle East. Eisenhower was content with British domination, but when the Soviets became active in the area, he felt that "the United States could no longer remain a silent partner." "We had to step in," he commented in his memoirs, "to counter the weight of Soviet power." In a message to the British, he explained that the United States could not be "acquiescent in any measure which would give the Bear's claws a grip on the production or transportation of oil which is so vital to the defence and economy of the Western world."[12] The first move came in February 1955 when the United States and

England completed arrangements for the formation of the Baghdad Pact, consisting of Turkey, Iran, Pakistan, and Iraq, along with Britain, to serve as a bulwark to block Soviet advance into this sensitive area. Secretary Dulles saw this "northern tier" as one more step in his policy of surrounding Russia with Western alliance systems, but he withheld American participation for fear of antagonizing other Arab states.

President Gamel Abdel Nasser of Egypt reacted strongly against the formation of the Baghdad Pact, particularly since it aligned the rival Arab state of Iraq with the Western powers. Smarting also over recent French arms sales to Israel, Nasser retaliated in the fall of 1955 by signing an arms deal with the Soviet Union, disguised in the form of a transaction with Czechoslovakia. Realizing that the Baghdad Pact had now opened the way for Soviet penetration of the Middle East, the United States and Britain responded by entering into negotiations to help Nasser finance his ambitious Aswan Dam—a great hydro-electric and irrigation project on the Nile River that the Egyptian leader had made the centerpiece for his nation's modernization. In December 1955, they reached agreement on a preliminary financing package under which the United States would supply $56 million and the British $14 million to pay for the initial engineering work, with the World Bank to underwrite an additional $200 million for the actual construction of the dam. There were provisions for further Anglo-American grants of up to $200 million, but these were clearly dependent on future political cooperation on Nasser's part.

Western relations with Egypt steadily deteriorated during the spring of 1956. Nasser resented some of the conditions placed on the Egyptian economy in the Aswan financial package. In Congress, Southern members expressed concern over aiding a project that would add to the world's cotton supply, while supporters of Israel were reluctant to aid that nation's leading enemy. Then in May, Nasser recognized Communist China, an act that outraged John Foster Dulles, raising, as he later put it, the issue of whether "nations which play both sides get better treatment than nations which are stalwart and work with us." There was no question in the secretary's mind of the answer, and when the Soviets indicated that they were now interested in financing the Aswan Dam, Dulles was ready to withdraw the American offer. Before he acted, however, he consulted with President Eisenhower, who had been stricken with an attack of ileitis in early June. At a meeting of the National Security Council at Camp David on July 13, Eisenhower weighed all the factors involved, including the growing congressional opposition and recent British doubts, before he instructed Dulles to notify the Egyptians of the American withdrawal. The secretary did so at a meeting with the Egyptian ambassador in Washington on July 19, and afterwards drew the brunt of criticism for the consequences. The decision, however, was Eisenhower's, and the President never shirked the responsibility, writing in his memoirs, "I have never doubted the wisdom of canceling our offer."[13]

Nasser responded a week later with his nationalization of the Suez Canal, stating that he would operate the waterway efficiently and use the tolls to finance the Aswan Dam. Great Britain and France, America's two leading allies in Europe, reacted angrily and indicated that they could not accept Nasser's act. For the British, whose citizens owned most of the stock in the confiscated canal company, it was a humiliating blow to vital national interests. Anthony

Eden, who had finally succeeded Churchill as Prime Minister in 1955, likened Nasser to Hitler and Mussolini and vowed not to follow the path of appeasement. The French, who viewed Nasser as the cause of their Algerian troubles, saw a chance to topple him from power. Eisenhower took a broader view. His concern was not with Nasser, but with the effect of the canal seizure on Western Europe. If Nasser proved that he could run the canal smoothly, as the President thought likely, then a peaceful solution would be possible. Calling the canal "the world's foremost public utility," Eisenhower realized that its closure "would seriously cripple Western Europe" by cutting off vital oil supplies and was therefore "unthinkable." He arranged for the creation of a Middle East Emergency Committee, composed of government officials and representatives of the major oil companies, to prepare ways to supply Europe with oil if Egypt blocked the normal shipments from the Persian Gulf by closing the canal.[14]

Throughout the ensuing crisis, Eisenhower repeatedly ruled out a military solution. "I can't conceive of military force being a good solution," he told the press on August 8. In his communications to Anthony Eden, he was even more adamant. He told the British leader on July 31 that the "drastic means" Eden was contemplating should not be used until "every peaceful means of resolving the difficulty had previously been exhausted." He explained his reasoning more fully on September 2 when he told the Prime Minister, "I really do not see how a successful result could be achieved by forcible means." "The use of force," he continued, "would it seems to me, vastly increase the area of jeopardy." He kept warning of the danger of flouting world opinion and of driving the Arabs into the arms of the Soviet Union. Unlike the British and French, Ike was not intent on overthrowing Nasser. His concern was with the global implications of Suez, especially with the loss of Middle Eastern oil during a war to capture the canal and the opportunity such a venture would present to "the Russians to make mischief."[15]

Dulles, however, viewed the crisis in the context of the presidential campaign, so he directed all his efforts toward postponing a showdown until after the election in November. Thus Townsend Hoopes describes Dulles's diplomacy as designed to "buy time for Eisenhower's reelection," and suggests that the secretary of state secretly wanted the British to bring Nasser down once the election was over. The President, however, genuinely believed that force was inappropriate in this situation. He was responding not so much to the possible political impact at home as to the effect on world opinion. He worried about alienating "the people of the Near East and of North Africa and, to some extent, of all of Asia and all of Africa." He was willing to contemplate military action only in the event that Nasser closed the canal, stating that "the fate of Western Europe must never be placed at the whim of a dictator."[16] But he realized above all that the crisis transcended Nasser and involved the risk of Soviet domination of the Middle East. Such a situation required skillful diplomacy and self-restraint, not a show of force.

II

Despite his different perception of the crisis, Dulles tried hard to carry out Eisenhower's prudent policy. In August 1956 he went to London to attend a 24-nation conference at which he presented a plan for creating an international authority to manage the canal. When Nasser rejected this proposal in early September, England and France were well along in their preparations for an invasion of Egypt, scheduled for mid-September. In desperation, Dulles devised the idea of a Suez Canal Users Association and prevailed upon Eden to convene a second conference in London to discuss this idea, which would prove to be equally distasteful to Nasser. The British and French, already upset by these delaying tactics, became angry when the secretary told a press conference that "we do not intend to shoot our way through" but would instead go around the Cape of Good Hope if Nasser closed the canal. The failure of the Second London Conference convinced the European allies that they would have to devise their own solution to the Suez crisis without further consultation with the United States.[17]

In October, with the French taking the lead, England and France entered into a secret agreement with Israel. On October 29, the Israelis would launch an attack on the Sinai aimed at the Gaza Strip, where the Egyptians had permitted Arab terrorists to conduct raids, and at Sharm el-Sheikh, key to the Egyptian blockade of the Gulf of Aqaba. The British and French, pretending surprise, would respond on October 30 with an ultimatum demanding that both Israel and Egypt withdraw within twelve hours from the area of the Suez Canal. With the expected Egyptian refusal, England and France would then send in troops to seize the canal on the pretext of preserving the neutrality of the waterway during the Israeli-Egyptian fighting. The British had wanted to postpone the operation until after the American election, but the French insisted on acting immediately. Leaders of both nations, however, expected the United States to accept their action as a *fait accompli*.[18]

Eisenhower was in the midst of a campaign swing through the South when the news arrived of the Israeli attack on October 29. He hurried back to Washington and informed his principal national security advisers that he would honor the Tripartite Declaration of 1950 opposing the use of force between Israel and her Arab neighbors and thus seek an immediate cease-fire. He instructed Dulles to inform the Israelis that "goddam it, we're going to apply sanctions, we're going to the United Nations, we're going to do everything that there is so we can stop this thing." He then called in the British chargé d'affaires and told him that he expected the British to honor their obligations under the Tripartite Declaration. When the British diplomat asked what the United States planned to do, Ike replied, "We plan to get to the United Nations the first thing in the morning. When the door opens. Before the USSR gets there."[19]

The President was furious the next day when he learned of the British-French ultimatum and realized that it was the prelude to an invasion. "The White House crackled with barracks-room language," reported one observer as the President gave vent to his anger at the British and the French. When the ultimatum expired and the British began bombing Egyptian bases on October 31, Eisenhower expressed his amazement at the rashness of Anthony Eden. "Bombs, by God," he exploded. "What does Anthony think he's doing?" He telephoned Eden to express his "deep concern" over British policy and proceeded to give the Prime Minister a "tongue-lashing" that reduced him to tears. Privately, Eisenhower expressed his amazement at the way the British and French were making

"Such a complete *mess* and *botch* of things." He told Emmet Hughes that it was "the damnedest business I ever saw supposedly intelligent governments get themselves into."[20]

At the United Nations, England and France vetoed the Security Council resolution calling for a cease-fire. Eisenhower replied with a speech in which he voiced his belief that "there can be no peace—without law" and then added "And there can be no law—if we were to invoke one code of international conduct for those who oppose us—and another for our friends." Dulles then took the American cease-fire resolution to the General Assembly, where there was no veto, and with the uninvited support of the Soviet Union, finally secured a call for England, France, and Israel to halt their invasion of Egypt by a vote of 64 to 5.[21]

On Sunday, November 4, the Israelis heeded the UN and halted their operations in the Sinai. Striking with speed and precision, they had fulfilled all their objectives, taking control of the Gaza Strip and lifting the blockade of the Gulf of Aqaba with the capture of Sharm el-Sheikh. The British and French were not so successful. For six days they bombed Egyptian bases while they mounted their forces in the Mediterranean. Finally their paratroopers jumped from the skies over the canal on November 5, and the next day the first ground troops landed in Egypt. Nasser's forces put up stiff resistance at Port Said, thereby denying the European powers the quick victory they needed. Meanwhile, as Eisenhower had warned, world opinion turned against the Western powers and allowed the Soviet Union to exploit the situation. On November 5, Marshal Nikolai Bulganin sent messages to England and France denouncing their attack on Egypt and threatening rocket attacks against their cities if the invasion continued.

At this point, Eisenhower took personal charge of the crisis. Dulles had been stricken on November 3 with the first symptoms of the stomach cancer that would eventually take his life; he entered Walter Reed Hospital for an operation that kept him away from his office for two months. With the election on November 6, the President ignored the campaign entirely and concentrated on the new danger posed by the Soviet Union. In a separate message to the United States on November 5, Bulganin warned Eisenhower that the fighting in the Middle East could lead to a "world war" and suggested that the United States join with the Soviet Union in military action designed to curb the aggression by England, France, and Israel. Eisenhower angrily rejected the Russian proposal, calling it "unthinkable." Ike was convinced that the Russians were bluffing, but he took no chances, placing American forces on a worldwide alert. As he recalled later, "we just told them [the Russians] that this would be, well, we just told them, really, it would be global war if they started it, that's all."[22]

"It would be difficult to exaggerate the extreme tension that gripped the United States Government between about 6 o'clock last night and 1 o'clock this afternoon," commented the New York *Times* on election day. "It goes without saying that the thought of nuclear war was urgently in many minds." Emmet Hughes recalls the President telling him that "if those fellows start something, we may have to hit 'em—and, if necessary, with *everything* in the bucket." Eisenhower confirmed the seriousness of the situation in his memoirs where he recalls telling Allen Dulles, "If the Soviets should attack Britain and France directly, we would of course be in a major war."[23]

Eisenhower's estimate of Soviet intentions was never put to the test. Early on the morning of November 6, Anthony Eden finally decided to heed the UN resolution and halt the invasion. Many factors influenced his decision, including a sharp decline in Britain's dollar reserves which the United States refused to stem while the fighting continued. Eden informed the President of the cease-fire order in a trans-Atlantic telephone conversation around noon on November 6, and at the end of the call politely inquired about the American election. "I don't give a darn about the election," Ike replied, and then added, "I guess it will be all right."[24]

In fact, the crisis atmosphere helped ensure the President's re-election by a commanding majority. Eisenhower was undoubtedly sincere when he said that he had forgotten all about politics in the midst of the war scare. His main regret was that his analysis of the situation had been so accurate. The foolish resort to force by England and France had turned world opinion against them and had enabled the Soviets to come forth as the protector of Egypt. The President realized that now the United States would have to fill the vacuum created by the withdrawal of England and France from this vital area of the world. Although much of the controversy and debate surrounding American policy in the crisis would focus on John Foster Dulles, the secretary of state had in fact played a subordinate role throughout. His brother, CIA director Allen Dulles, commented to a colleague, "Don't you realize that the individual who was really furious with the British and French and absolutely insistent on the action we took was Eisenhower not Foster?"[25] The President called the shots, and his only mistake was to permit his secretary of state to convey to the British the impression that the United States would look the other way when they launched their invasion.

III

In the months that followed the cease-fire on November 7, 1956, President Eisenhower sought to restore order in the Middle East. His policy had two clear goals. The first was short-range and manageable—persuade the British, French, and Israelis to withdraw from the Egyptian territory they had seized. The second was long-range and less easily attained—prevent the Soviets from exploiting the British and French defeat to expand their influence in the Middle East. Eisenhower's pursuit of these two goals required a new and vigorous American policy in an area previously considered a preserve of our European allies.

The situation following the cease-fire was very confused. Israel was in good shape, with its forces in control of the Gaza Strip and Sharm el-Sheikh; the British and French were in an awkward position, controlling Port Said at the north end of the canal, which Nasser had blocked with forty scuttled ships when the fighting began. The United Nations was preparing to send in an emergency force to occupy the canal area and permit the evacuation of the European troops. Meanwhile, the canal closure, coupled with the sabotage of the main pipeline from the Persian Gulf to the Mediterranean, had created a serious oil shortage in Western Europe. England and France normally relied on the Middle East for 75 per cent of their petroleum; unless they received emergency shipments from the United States, they would soon run out of gasoline for their cars, heat for their homes, and energy for their factories.

The Eisenhower administration decided to take advantage of this oil crunch. Although the President at first had wanted to invite Eden to Washington for a conference, State Department officials finally persuaded him to hew to a hard line. The United States, the President declared, could offer no assistance to England and France until they withdrew their troops from the canal area. Instead of convening the Middle East Emergency Committee to arrange for the transfer of Western Hemisphere oil to Europe, Eisenhower deliberately suspended this government-industry effort, despite protests from American oil companies. A dismayed Anthony Eden admitted that he had not foreseen that "The United States Government would harden against us on almost every point and become harsher after the cease-fire than before." Deprived of petroleum, England and France had no choice but to give in. Assured that the requested evacuation would take place soon, the President on November 30 authorized the beginning of an oil lift to Western Europe whereby fifteen American companies arranged for the shipment of 500,000 barrels of oil a day, partly from increased American and Venezuelan production, partly from a diversion of Persian Gulf oil. Three days later, the British announced that they would remove their troops from Egypt, and on December 22 the last English and French units left the canal area, thus ending the disastrous Suez expedition.[26]

The President was deeply concerned with the possibility of Soviet advance into the area as the British and French left. He conferred with a recuperating John Foster Dulles on this problem in December, and then he and the secretary shared their conclusions with a small group of congressional leaders at a New Year's Day meeting at the White House. "The existing vacuum in the Middle East," Eisenhower declared, "must be filled by the United States before it is filled by Russia." He went on to explain that he planned to ask Congress for a special economic fund to aid Arab nations threatened by communism and for authority to use force to repel Soviet aggression. The congressmen and senators were dubious about the new commitment, expressing reservations over the use of force. The President assured them he would not act without specific congressional approval and only on the request of a Middle Eastern country, adding that if the authority were granted, "it might never have to be used." Eisenhower conceded that he had the power to act on his own in an emergency, but he wanted Congress to help him "make our intent clear in advance."[27]

The President submitted his formal request to Congress in a special message on January 5, 1957. "Russia's rulers have long sought to dominate the Middle East," he began. "This was true of the Czars and it is true of the Bolsheviks. . . ." Then he laid out what soon became known as the Eisenhower Doctrine, a three-part grant of authority for presidential action in the Middle East. First, he asked for $200 million in economic assistance to preserve the independence of "any nation or group of nations in the general area of the Middle East"; second, he requested military assistance for the same countries; finally, he called on Congress to permit him to use the armed forces to protect Middle Eastern nations "requesting such aid" against "overt armed aggression from any nation controlled by International Communism."[28]

Critics quickly pointed out the weaknesses in the Eisenhower Doctrine. Soviet penetration was most likely in Egypt and Syria, nations unlikely to request aid from the United States. The main threat to the independence of pro-Western countries, such as Jordan and Lebanon, came from the rising strength of Arab nationalism, personified by Nasser, and not from "International Communism." Most Arab spokesmen warned the United States to stay out of the Middle East, vowing that they could solve their problems without American help. Even at home, there was doubt, with Dean Acheson dismissing the Eisenhower Doctrine as "vague, inadequate and not very helpful."[29]

Despite this reaction, the President did not waver. In a letter to Churchill in November 1956, Eisenhower had expressed the sorrow he felt over opposing Britain on Suez, and then had added, "The Soviets are the real enemy of the Western World, implacably hostile and seeking our destruction." He firmly believed that they "had their eyes on the Middle East," and that if the United States did not stand squarely in Russia's path, communism would sweep over the entire area. In particular, the President worried about Soviet designs on Persian Gulf oil, claiming that they did not need this precious resource for themselves but rather planned "to seize the oil, to cut the canal and the pipelines of the Middle East, and thus seriously to weaken Western civilization." Eisenhower was apparently convinced that it was an American obligation to block "the Soviet Union's march . . . to the underground lakes of oil which fuel the homes and factories of Western Europe." Having just exploited this vulnerability to effect British and French withdrawal from Suez, the President was especially sensitive to the importance of petroleum to the world economy.[30]

IV

Congress did not share Eisenhower's sense of urgency over the Middle East resolution. The House acted promptly, voting 355 to 61 for the authority which the President had requested. But in the Senate doubts about extending aid to Arab nations troubled supporters of Israel, while the Democratic leadership, still smarting from Eisenhower's re-election, insisted on modifying the administration's resolution. Senator Lyndon Johnson was successful in amending the legislation to deny a specific authorization for the use of troops; instead, the Senate simply stated that the United States "is prepared" to employ force if the President "determines the necessity thereof."[31]

Despite Dulles's objection, the President had agreed to the new wording when a new problem in the Middle East postponed further action on the Eisenhower Doctrine. The Israelis had withdrawn their troops from most of the Sinai in November, but they continued to hold two key areas—the Gaza Strip and Sharm el-Sheikh. In February 1957, Prime Minister David Ben Gurion declared that Israel would insist on maintaining police power in Gaza to prevent a recurrence of Arab terrorist raids and on retaining the strategic post that controlled access to the Gulf of Aqaba and the port of Elath. Egypt refused to reopen the Suez Canal while Israel occupied portions of the Sinai, thereby intensifying the continued oil shortage in Western Europe, which had been only partially alleviated by the American oil lift. A worried Eisenhower, declaring that "We must not allow Europe to go flat on its back for the want of oil," decided now to back UN efforts to apply economic sanctions against Israel to compel a full withdrawal from Gaza and Sharm el-Sheikh. Senate Majority Leader Lyndon Johnson, however, immediately raised an objection to American pressure against Israel. In a letter to Dulles, Johnson asked the secretary to instruct the American delegation to the United Nations to oppose

93

"with all its skill" any attempt to impose sanctions on Israel. There clearly would be no further Senate action on the Eisenhower Doctrine until the threat against Israel was removed.[32]

Dulles flew to Georgia, where the President was vacationing at Secretary of the Treasury George Humphrey's hunting lodge. Informed of the Senate objections, Eisenhower was insistent on applying economic pressure on Israel, even to the extent of cutting off private American assistance, estimated to run at over $100 million a year. Then he agreed to cut short his vacation and return to Washington for a showdown with the Senate leaders.

The resulting White House conference on February 20 was long and angry. The President tried to impress upon the congressional leaders the vital need to reopen the Suez Canal and resume the normal flow of oil. If the United States permitted Israel to retain territory it had conquered, Eisenhower warned, the result would be "increased influence of Russia in the Arab states," "interruption of the flow of oil," "possibly a serious crash in the French and United Kingdom economies and, finally, an increased possibility of general war." Neither Lyndon Johnson nor Senate Minority Leader William Knowland was impressed, and it soon became clear that the Senate would not cooperate in imposing sanctions against Israel. Eisenhower could not believe that domestic political considerations "could enter so much into life-or-death, peace-or-war decisions." He finally told the congressmen and senators that he would take the issue to the American people. House Speaker Sam Rayburn approved, commenting, "America has either one voice or none, and that voice is the voice of the President—whether everybody agrees with him or not."[33]

That evening the President spoke to the nation by radio and television. "The future of the United Nations and peace in the Middle East may be at stake," he began, and then proceeded to outline the Israeli refusal to withdraw and the United Nations plan for economic sanctions. "If we agree that armed attack can properly achieve the purposes of the assailant," Eisenhower declared, "then I fear we will have turned back the clock of international order." He then stated his belief that the United Nations had "no choice but to exert pressure upon Israel," and indicated that he would cooperate in this effort.[34]

The President's firm stand finally convinced the Israelis. During the last week of February, several intermediaries, including French Foreign Minister Christian Pineau and Canadian Foreign Minister Lester Pearson, worked out a compromise whereby the United Nations Emergency Force would occupy both Gaza and Sharm el-Sheikh. President Eisenhower, in addition, reaffirmed an earlier American pledge to uphold "the right of free and innocent passage" of the Gulf of Aqaba and "to join with others to secure general recognition of this right." Accordingly, on March 1, 1957, Golda Meir, the Israeli foreign minister, informed the UN General Assembly of her nation's plans for a total withdrawal of troops from the disputed areas.[35]

The logjam then broke quickly. On March 2, Senator Johnson defeated an amendment to eliminate references to economic and military assistance from the Eisenhower Doctrine; a week later, the Senate passed the resolution by the comfortable margin of 58 to 28. The last detachment of Israeli troops left the Sinai on March 6, surrendering their positions to the UN Emergency Force. Finally, the Suez Canal reopened on March 29 when a convoy of nine freighters made the first passage since October 1956. Once again oil flowed by tanker through the canal, thus relieving the intense fuel shortage in Western Europe. Best of all for the President, the Israeli withdrawal had ended the danger of a showdown between the executive and legislative branches over economic sanctions.

It is difficult to decide if anyone emerged victorious from the long and debilitating Suez crisis. Nasser became a hero in the Arab world, but his army had been soundly defeated by the Israelis and his country had met with serious economic reverses during the canal's closure. The Russians had undoubtedly increased their influence in the Middle East, but they had never shown the ambition attributed to them by Eisenhower and Dulles, and they were very cautious in the face of the prevailing Arab nationalism. Peter Lyon argues that the Eisenhower administration was the only "winner," since the United States had come out of the Suez fiasco as the "presumptive protector of the Middle East" and the guardian of the oil so vital to Western Europe.[36] Certainly from this time forward, the United States would be the dominant Western influence in the area, and American companies would control an ever-greater portion of the Persian Gulf oil in the days before OPEC. Eisenhower had succeeded in his goal of filling the vacuum in the Middle East, replacing England and France there just as in 1954 he had supplanted the French in Indochina. Yet the price was also great—alienation of the nation's oldest and most reliable allies. There is great irony in the fact that Eisenhower, the man hailed as the savior of Western Europe in World War II, would become the president who extended American power and influence globally at the expense of England and France.

V

In the aftermath of Suez, Eisenhower found it difficult to restore order and stability to the troubled Middle East. He was able to employ the Eisenhower Doctrine effectively in the spring of 1957 to support King Hussein in Jordan. An emergency grant of $10 million and the shift of the Sixth Fleet to the eastern Mediterranean enabled that pro-Western ruler to beat back a nationalist threat to his throne. In the fall, growing Soviet influence in Syria led to yet another crisis in which the United States, attempting to work through Iraq and Turkey, proved unable to influence the course of events. The danger of Soviet dominance in Syria ended in February when Nasser agreed to join that country with Egypt to form the United Arab Republic. Nasser quickly outlawed the Communist party but created a new threat to stability by putting pressure on tiny Lebanon to join with Egypt and Syria in a larger Arab federation.

Lebanon had emerged from French rule after World War II as a predominantly Arab country with a population nearly evenly divided between Maronite Christians and Sunni Moslems. A carefully constructed National Pact split political control between these two religious groups, with the Christians controlling the presidency and foreign ministry and the Moslems the parliament. Lebanon had pursued a neutralist foreign policy until the time of the Suez crisis, but then President Camille Chamoun had angered the Moslem faction by embracing the Eisenhower Doctrine and adopting a pro-Western stance. With his six-year term as President due to expire later in 1958, Chamoun began to maneuver for a change in the constitution to permit his re-election. In May, civil unrest broke out as the Moslem population, encouraged by a constant propaganda barrage from Radio Cairo, vowed to prevent Chamoun from securing another term in office. Troops and supplies flowed in across the mountains from Syria, while General Fuad Chehab, the Christian army commander, averted bloodshed by refusing to attack the rebels. Finally, on May 13, a worried Chamoun appealed to Eisenhower, asking what his response would be if Lebanon were to request American assistance.[37]

The President was genuinely perplexed. He realized that Chamoun had committed "a political error" in working for a second term, but at the same time he was convinced that "the Communists were principally responsible for the trouble" in Lebanon. Dulles had no doubts about the need to send troops, although he did warn that armed American intervention would probably cause "a wave of resentment among the Arab populations" and lead to pipeline sabotage and possible closure of the Suez Canal. Dulles also mentioned the possibility of a Russian response, but Ike discounted this, commenting, "I believed the Soviets would not take action if the United States movement were decisive and strong." In the end, however, Eisenhower's instinctive caution won out. He told Chamoun that the United States would intervene only if a second Arab state backed Lebanon's request for American troops and if it was clear that the intervention was not designed to secure another term for Chamoun. For the time being, the United States urged Lebanon to take its complaints against the United Arab Republic to the UN and for Chamoun to deal with the local disturbances "with his own forces." American involvement, Eisenhower felt, "should be a last resort."[38]

The crisis in Lebanon eased in June as United Nations observers entered the country and found little evidence of direct Egyptian and Syrian involvement in the domestic unrest. The possibility of American intervention seemed to be fading when suddenly a dramatic coup in Iraq changed the situation radically. On the evening of July 13, forces led by General Abdul Karim Kassem entered the royal palace in Baghdad and killed young King Faisal II and Crown Prince Abdulillah. The pro-Western Prime Minister, Nuri as-Said, escaped, but the next day the rebels captured and killed him, and then let a mob drag his body through the streets of the capital. The CIA was caught completely by surprise. No one in Washington had any inkling of the coup nor any indication of whether either the Soviet Union or the United Arab Republic was behind General Kassem. But the brutal overthrow of a friendly Arab government and the apparent loss of a key member of the Baghdad Pact created a deep sense of crisis.[39]

The President was at his desk at 7:30 on the morning of July 14 to deal with the new situation. Shaken by the Iraqi revolt, Eisenhower was equally concerned over the possibility of a coup in Lebanon. When President Chamoun sent an urgent appeal for American help, Ike was ready to act. In the course of the day, he went through the ritual of consulting the National Security Council and a bipartisan congressional delegation. Those around him remarked on how calm and relaxed he appeared at these meetings. At the morning session of the NSC he barely let Secretary Dulles explain the options, interrupting him to say, "Foster, I've already made up my mind. We're going in." His only concern was with the military details. "How soon can you start, Nate?" he asked General Nathan Twining, chairman of the Joint Chiefs. When Twining replied,

99

"Fifteen minutes after I get back to the Pentagon," Ike commented, "Well, what are we waiting for?"[40]

The congressional leaders were skeptical of the need to use force, but when Eisenhower indicated that he would take full responsibility, they quickly fell in line. For the President, the issue was clear cut. Unless there was a "vigorous response" by the United States, the loss of Iraq could lead to "a complete elimination of Western influence in the Middle East." He felt a compelling need, as he explained to Robert Murphy, to dispel the Arab belief that "Americans were capable only of words, that we were afraid of Soviet reaction if we attempted military action." His conviction that there was no choice, that "we had to go in," explains the calm manner that so impressed his associates on July 14. Robert Cutler took pride in "an experienced Commander in Chief who knew what to do."[41]

The American landings, which began the next day, embodied the restrained and careful use of force that Eisenhower favored. A detachment of marines from the Sixth Fleet moved in swiftly across the beaches and secured the Beirut airport, then joined the American ambassador and General Chehab, who escorted them into the capital. Army units from West Germany, complete with tanks and Honest John atomic cannons, arrived by air shortly afterwards. Within three days, over 7000 American troops were in Lebanon without a shot being fired; the force would eventually grow to more than 14,000. Eisenhower was careful to describe the action as a "garrison move" and not an invasion. The mission of the American troops was "not primarily to fight," Eisenhower explained later, but to show the flag. The President overruled the military, who wanted to occupy all Lebanon, and restricted American activity to Beirut and the adjoining airport. All that Eisenhower wanted to do was to convince the Arab nations that the United States was prepared to defend its interests in the Middle East; political influence, not military victory, was the desired goal.[42]

The President was less than candid with the American people. On July 15, he had James Hagerty release a statement justifying the intervention on grounds of protecting American citizens in Lebanon and in maintaining the integrity of the Lebanese government. In an evening television speech to the nation, he shifted to a traditional Cold War rationale, likening the situation in Lebanon to the Communist threat to Greece in 1947, Czechoslovakia in 1948, China in 1949, Korea in 1950, and Indochina in 1954. Lebanon, he suggested, was about to become the victim of indirect Communist aggression, and thus he was acting to stem the Soviet tide. Yet there was no evidence of Russian activity in Lebanon; the problem was essentially internal, with understandable Moslem anxiety over Chamoun's political maneuvers intensified by Nasser's propaganda. Arab nationalism, not Soviet communism, was the source of danger to American hopes for a stable Middle East.[43]

The President apparently understood the essence of the problem, even though he did not share his insights with the American people. His greatest concern was not a coup in Lebanon but rather the security of the Persian Gulf oil fields. He ordered the secretary of the interior to reform the Middle East Emergency Committee, composed of government officials and representatives of private oil companies, and charged it with making plans for another oil lift to Western Europe. Worried about a possible Iraqi move against Kuwait, he transferred a Marine regimental combat team from Okinawa to the Persian Gulf and moved a tactical air strike force from Europe to bases in Turkey. Convinced that the security of Western Europe depended on the flow of oil from the Middle East, Eisenhower wanted to impress the Arab leaders with American resolve. Nor was he bluffing. "Finally, I instructed General Twining," he commented in his memoirs, "to be prepared to employ, subject to my personal approval, *whatever* means might become necessary to prevent any unfriendly forces from moving into Kuwait."

The President's determination to make Lebanon a display of American resolve in the Middle East impressed Arab leaders. General Kassem was quick to assure the European nations that there would be no interruption in the flow of oil, announcing on Baghdad radio on July 18 the "continued production and export of oil to world markets." The Middle East Emergency Committee never had to activate its plans for an oil lift, and Dulles's fears of pipeline sabotage and blockage of the Suez Canal did not materialize.[44]

In Lebanon, Robert Murphy, a veteran diplomat whom Eisenhower sent to Beirut as his personal envoy, quickly arranged a settlement that satisfied both religious factions. On July 31, the Parliament selected General Chehab as the next President, to succeed Chamoun when his term expired in the fall. Chehab took office in September, and the next month the last American units left Lebanon. The 102-day occupation could have been avoided if Chamoun had been willing to accept Chehab as his successor in the spring; the irony is that Nasser had proposed precisely that solution in April.[45]

If Eisenhower's intervention was not really necessary to save Lebanon, it did serve a broader purpose, one that was uppermost in the President's mind. American credibility was at stake in the Middle East in the anxious period following the Suez debacle. Despite the Eisenhower Doctrine, events in the area were moving, as Ike viewed them, "toward chaos." In Lebanon, the choice was between antagonizing the Arab nations and risking war with Russia on the one hand, or "something worse—which was to do nothing." Nor was the President thinking only of the Middle East. "He wanted to demonstrate in a timely and practical way," Murphy recalls, "that the United States was capable of supporting its friends." Dulles made the same point at a cabinet meeting on July 18, explaining that he and the President were using force not just to "prevent the dangerous situation in the Middle East from getting any worse," but also "to reassure many small nations that they could call on us in time of crisis." Thus for the Eisenhower administration Lebanon was an opportunity to use limited force to restore Western influence and prestige.[46]

There is certainly room for criticism of Eisenhower's action in Lebanon, but Peter Lyon goes too far when he claims that the President had in mind a "forcible counterrevolution in Iraq."[47] Miscalculating the number of troops involved, Lyon fails to understand that the intervention in Lebanon was designed to impress Arab leaders with American strength and determination, not incite their opponents to overthrow them. General Kassem understood the meaning of American policy in Lebanon quite clearly. Eisenhower was concerned above all with the dependence of Western Europe on Middle Eastern oil, and thus his action in Lebanon flowed from the same fundamental concern as his policies in Iran in 1953 and during the Suez crisis in 1956. The general who had won his reputation by waging mechanized warfare with planes and tanks to liberate Europe in World War II knew how vital petroleum was for both the military defense and the peacetime economy of America's closest allies. If at times he confused the danger from Arab nationalism with that from Soviet communism, at least he had a clear sense of the strategic value of Persian Gulf oil and acted boldly to protect that vital national interest.

4 / Eisenhower and the Russians

The crises in Asia and the Middle East took up much of Eisenhower's time in the 1950s, but they never diverted the President from the overriding aim of his foreign policy—reducing Cold War tensions and achieving détente with the Soviet Union. Ike's pursuit of peace was the dominant feature of his presidency, and the failure to secure it his greatest disappointment. This quest was flawed by Eisenhower's uncritical assumption that the Cold War was the result of Russian fear and hostility. He believed that all he had to do was to convince the men in the Kremlin that the United States was not out to encircle or destroy the Soviet Union. Hoping to gain their trust, he believed he could reverse their belligerence and persuade them to accept Western solutions to such fundamental problems as the future of Germany, the division of Europe and, above all, the nuclear arms race.

It is easy to condemn Eisenhower for holding such a naive view of the complicated world situation of the 1950s, yet his very innocence gave him a global appeal that no other postwar American leader could match. Whether by design or not, Ike pursued a series of peaceful initiatives from the White House that contrasted sharply with the suspicious and aggressive policies that Dulles propounded in the State Department. The result was to give American policy a schizophrenic appearance, with the secretary of state waging a Cold War and the President searching for détente. The hard line that Dulles favored reassured fervent anti-Communists at home and in Congress, while Eisenhower's more pacific overtures appealed to the hopes of men everywhere for genuine peace.

I

Eisenhower's first attempt to grapple with the Russian issue came early in his first term, with the death of Joseph Stalin on March 5, 1953. When news that the Soviet leader had suffered a stroke reached the President the morning before his death, he inquired of his advisers tartly, "Well, what do you think we can do about *this?*" Dulles cautioned against any immediate statement, but finally the President authorized a bland expression of sympathy addressed to the Russian people. In a cabinet meeting three days later, Eisenhower expressed his amazement that the State Department had never devised a contingency measure for this momentous occasion. "We have no plan," Ike exclaimed. "We are not even sure what difference his death makes."[1]

The statements issued by the new Soviet leader, Georgi Malenkov, indicated that the Russians might be receptive to peaceful overtures from the United States. At Stalin's funeral, Malenkov spoke of "peaceful coexistence and competition" with the United States. Later in March, Malenkov announced to the Supreme Soviet that "there is not one disputed or undecided question that cannot be decided by peaceful means on the basis of mutual understanding of interested countries." To the cheers of his audience, he added, "This is our attitude toward all states, among them the U.S.A."[2]

Dulles reacted warily to this new Soviet line. He warned the President that the Russians were simply trying to cover up their internal weaknesses and recommended a policy of increased pressure. Eisenhower, however, was more hopeful. In late March, he told Emmet Hughes that he was thinking of making a major foreign policy address in which he would respond to Malenkov's remarks. "Look," the President exclaimed, "I am tired—and I think everyone is tired—of just plain indictments of the Soviet regime." Instead of condemning the Russians, he explained to Hughes, he wanted to give a speech in which he made a series of specific peaceful proposals and then challenged the Russians to respond to them. "The past speaks for itself," he told Hughes. "I am interested in the future. Both their government and ours now have new men in them. The slate is clean. Now let us begin talking to each other."[3]

For the next three weeks, Hughes tried his best to prepare a speech that captured Eisenhower's enthusiasm for a new departure in the Cold War. John Foster Dulles continually expressed his skepticism as Hughes prepared draft after draft, but finally the President approved a text that bore out many of his original ideas. Scheduled for delivery before the American Society of Newspaper Editors on April 16, 1953, the speech nearly went undelivered. Eisenhower awoke that morning with severe stomach cramps (a forerunner of the ileitis attack he would suffer in 1956), but he insisted on going ahead. As he spoke to the editors that day, the cramps returned, sending chills through his body and making the words swim before his eyes. He hurried through the last few paragraphs, leaving out details and speeding up his delivery, but gamely finishing.

The words had an eloquence rare in Eisenhower's addresses. He began by citing the cost of eight years of Cold War: "Every gun that is made, every warship launched, every rocket fired signifies, in the final sense, a theft from those who hunger and are not fed, those who are cold and are not clothed." "This is not a way of life at all, in any true sense," the President continued. "Under the cloud of threatening war, it is humanity hanging from a cross of iron." He then called upon the Soviets to take a few "clear and specific steps" to demonstrate their sincerity, such as signing an Austrian peace treaty, concluding an armistice in Korea, agreeing to free elections for the reunification of Germany, and restoring freedom to Eastern Europe. Then he closed with a plea for nuclear disarmament, repeating proposals long rejected by the Soviets, and promising that the United States would dedicate a portion of the savings from disarmament "to a fund for world aid and reconstruction" so that America could serve "the *needs*, rather than the *fears* of the world."[4]

There was a chorus of praise across the United States for Eisenhower's words, but the Russians quite understandably reacted coolly to his mixture of what two later observers called "new hope and Cold War gamesmanship." The President was asking the Soviets to give up all they had gained since World War II without offering anything more substantial in return than American goodwill. And yet the speech was more than an exercise in Cold War propaganda. Eisenhower genuinely believed that he had offered the Russians a chance for peace, and there could be no doubting the sincerity of his appeal. The April 16 speech embodied Eisenhower's belief that the United States "as a Free World leader . . . should always . . . display a spirit of firmness without truculence, conciliation without appeasement, confidence without arrogance."[5]

Winston Churchill responded to Eisenhower's speech on May 11 by calling for a summit conference with the Russians as soon as possible. Unlike the President, Churchill did not insist on specific deeds by the Soviets as proof of their good intentions. Urging a more flexible approach, the British leader declared, "It would be a mistake to assume that nothing could be settled with Soviet Russia unless or until everything is settled." Dulles, convinced that Malenkov had launched a "phony peace campaign," tried to halt what he considered an ill-fated rush to the summit. His main concern was the European Defense Community, a plan to rearm Germany by integrating its armed forces with those of the other Western nations on the continent. Fearful that the Russian peace overtures were simply a tactic to delay German rearmament, Dulles persuaded Ike to agree to meet only with the British and French at Bermuda to discuss a future summit. Churchill's failing health and a change in the French government forced postponement of the Bermuda conference until December and gave the secretary of state time to cool off the Western desire for a face-to-face meeting with the new Russian leaders.[6]

The Eisenhower administration may well have missed a genuine opportunity for détente in the months following Stalin's death. Malenkov appeared eager for a reduction in tensions, and in the issue of German rearmament the

Western powers had a valuable consideration to exploit in any bargain with the Russians. Charles Bohlen, the ambassador to Russia at the time, came to regret that Eisenhower did not "take up Churchill's call for a meeting at the summit." "I think I made a mistake," Bohlen confessed, "in not taking the initiative and recommending such a meeting." The opportunity soon passed. By 1954, Malenkov had fallen from power, to be replaced by Nikita Khrushchev, a far more formidable leader who preferred continued confrontation to any relaxation of tension. Yet given the grip of the Cold War on the American people and the sense of betrayal that any deal with the Russians would have engendered among right-wing Republicans still obsessed with memories of Yalta, Eisenhower's caution is understandable. Domestic constraints combined with Dulles's unshakeable suspicion of the Russians to leave the President content with his verbal appeal for peace and prevented him from engaging in more creative diplomacy in the spring of 1953.[7]

II

The nuclear arms race was by far the most ominous issue in Soviet-American relations in the mid-1950s, and the one that troubled Dwight Eisenhower the most. Just three days before his election in 1952, the United States had detonated its first thermonuclear device in the Pacific. The resulting explosion, nearly 1000 times larger than the atomic bomb that destroyed Hiroshima, wiped out an entire atoll, leaving only a huge crater in the ocean floor. Although the United States did not yet have a deliverable bomb (the device exploded in 1952 was as big as a two-story house and weighed sixty-five tons), the Atomic Energy Commission was perfecting America's first operational H-bomb. Most observers assumed that the Russians were pursuing the same goal.

As soon as he took office, Eisenhower searched for some way to bring home the awful realities of the nuclear age to the American people. Responding to the recommendations of a scientific panel headed by Robert Oppenheimer, he asked presidential assistant C. D. Jackson, his specialist in Cold War strategy, to prepare a speech informing the world of the new danger created by the hydrogen bomb. Dubbing his assignment Operation Candor, Jackson prepared draft after draft, only to have Eisenhower reject them on grounds that they were too somber and pessimistic. The President absorbed their contents, however, and in July, when he appointed Lewis Strauss to head the Atomic Energy Commission, he also asked him to serve as his personal adviser on nuclear issues. On the day that Strauss was sworn in, Eisenhower took him into the Oval Office in the White House and said: "Lewis, let us be certain about *this;* my chief concern and your first assignment is to find some new approach to the *dis*arming of atomic energy. . . . The world simply must not go on living in the fear of the terrible consequence of nuclear war."[8]

The President's concern deepened in August 1953 when he learned that the Russians had detonated their first hydrogen explosion in Siberia. On vacation in Denver, he recalled that Jackson's drafts had stressed the theme of human destruction, and thus would leave the listener "with only a new terror, not a new hope." Then Eisenhower hit upon a more promising approach, one that would offer a ray of hope. Returning to Washington in

September, he instructed National Security Adviser Robert Cutler to share his idea with C. D. Jackson and Lewis Strauss. Cutler promptly did so, asking these men to consider the following presidential proposal: "Suppose the United States and the Soviets were each to turn over to the United Nations for peaceful uses x kilograms of fissionable material. . . ." Jackson and Strauss reacted favorably, and despite the predictable skepticism of Dulles, the President told them to prepare the text of a speech that would combine the warning of destruction in Operation Candor with this new, more constructive proposal designed to appeal to mankind's instinct for survival.

Operation Wheaties, named for the breakfast session at which it was first discussed, dragged on for two more months as Strauss worked out the technical details of the proposal and Jackson labored through thirty-three different drafts of the presidential address. Eisenhower finally took the last draft with him to the Bermuda conference in early December to show to Churchill, who approved the concept but suggested a few final revisions. The President was scheduled to give the speech before the UN General Assembly in New York, and on the way back from Bermuda secretaries and statesmen alike worked aboard the presidential plane typing the final reading copy and mimeographing versions for the press. The security was so tight that Ambassador Bohlen, instructed to alert the Kremlin to the forthcoming speech, was not even told what it contained.[9]

On December 8 the President began the speech by reciting the horrors of nuclear war to the United Nations delegates. In somber tones, he described the "awful arithmetic" of the dread weapons, pointing out that atomic bombs had become twenty-five times more powerful than those used in 1945, while "hydrogen weapons are in the range of millions of tons of TNT equivalent." There was no defense against such weapons. A thermonuclear attack would "cause hideous damage" and lead to "the annihilation of the irreplaceable heritage of mankind." But then he began to outline a positive proposal. The nations possessing fissionable material should "begin now and continue to make joint contributions from their stockpiles . . . to an International Atomic Energy Agency." The United Nations should establish this new body, which would use the radioactive material to serve the needs of agriculture, medicine, and "to provide abundant electrical energy in the power-starved areas of the world." The United States "would be proud" to contribute to such a program, but of course the Soviet Union must also participate, the President insisted. The result, he concluded, would mean that "the contributing powers would be dedicating some of their strength to serve the needs rather than the fears of mankind. . . ."

It was a brilliant proposal that met with nearly universal praise. The General Assembly showered him with applause, with even the Communist delegates joining in. The press quickly labeled the new program "atoms for peace." Some cynics dismissed it as a public relations gimmick, while the Russians dragged their feet. But finally in 1957 the United Nations created the International Atomic Energy Agency and the "atoms for peace" program eventually was responsible for spreading the new technology around the world. Unfortunately, the safeguards proved inadequate, and the dissemination of fissionable materials contributed to the proliferation of nuclear weapons.[10]

Peter Lyon makes a more serious criticism of the "atoms for peace" speech, viewing it as purely "an exercise in psychological warfare." It is true, as Eisenhower admitted, that his own experts assured him that Soviet participation would be more damaging to their nuclear program, since "the United States could afford to reduce its atomic stockpile by two or three times the amount the Russians might contribute, and still improve our relative position." But Lyon misses Eisenhower's true purpose, which was to "promote development of mutual trust." Ever since the Russian rejection of the Baruch Plan in 1947, Soviet-American disarmament talks had been deadlocked over the issue of inspection. "Atoms for peace" was Eisenhower's attempt to get off "dead center," as he wrote his brother, by suggesting a small area of cooperation that "might expand into something broader." Above all, his speech to the General Assembly reflected his desire to probe for a way to brake the momentum of the nuclear arms race and find "specific ways by which future disaster can be avoided."[11]

Unfortunately, the President's words could not halt the technological process. On March 1, 1954, less then six months after his hopeful speech, the AEC detonated America's first deliverable H-bomb at Bikini atoll. The resulting explosion led to an unexpected cloud of deadly radioactivity that forced the United States to evacuate nearly 300 people on nearby islands. Twenty-three Japanese fishermen on board the *Lucky Dragon,* trolling some eighty miles from ground zero, were not so fortunate. Dusted with a silvery ash a few hours later, they wisely washed the unknown substance off their boat, but by the time they returned to Japan, they were all suffering from radioactive poisoning, and several months later one of them would die. Their plight heralded to the world the presence of a new and deadly by-product of the thermo-nuclear age: fallout.

The AEC had tried to throw a curtain of secrecy around the H-bomb test, but the fate of the *Lucky Dragon* led to rumors that the explosion had gotten out of control. Eisenhower finally asked Lewis Strauss to report on the March 1 test at his weekly presidential press conference on March 31, 1954. Strauss minimized the problem of fallout, explaining that most of it fell in the area already devastated by the shock and blast of the bomb. But then a reporter asked him if there were any upper limits on the size of an H-bomb. Strauss, without thinking, replied that "an H-bomb can be made as—large enough to take out a city." When startled reporters exclaimed "What?", Strauss reiterated, "To take out a city, to destroy a city." "How big a city?" a journalist asked; "Any city," Strauss replied. "Any city, New York?" shot back another reporter. "The metropolitan area, yes," the AEC chairman responded. Eisenhower then cut off the press conference, and on the way out he commented to Strauss, "Lewis, I wouldn't have answered that one that way."

The New York *Times* headline the next day read, "H-BOMB CAN WIPE OUT ANY CITY." Instead of quieting fears, Strauss's remarks focused the attention of the press on the frightening thought of single H-bombs destroying whole cities at one blow. Eisenhower, after checking with the Joint Chiefs of Staff, told a press conference on April 7 that there was "no military requirement that could lead us into the production of a bigger bomb than has already been produced." The public furor over fallout quickly subsided; people either decided the horror was beyond their capacity to contemplate or became involved in the other issues of the day, such as the Indochina crisis and the Army-McCarthy hearings.[12]

The President, however, could not escape the terrible dilemma created by the thermonuclear revolution. New Soviet tests in the fall of 1954 indicated that the Russians were approaching American proficiency in nuclear technology. Churchill's description of the peace of the world resting on "a balance of terror" was proving to be all too accurate. In a speech to a group of foreign service officers in October 1954, Eisenhower declared that there was no longer "any alternative to peace." "The soldier can no longer regain a peace that is usable to the world," he declared. All that he could produce through a resort to arms would be "a tattered nation that was very greatly in ashes and relics of destruction." He made the same point even more forcefully the next day when he told a college audience that "war does not present the possibility of victory or defeat. War would present to us only the alternatives in degrees of destruction."[13] Thus the President, by the end of his second year in office, had come to realize that his search for peace was not just desirable, but imperative. The reduction of tensions with the Soviet Union offered the only way that he could guarantee the security and well-being of his country.

III

Worldwide pressure for a summit conference had become irresistible by the spring of 1955. The issue of German rearmament, Dulles's greatest concern in 1953, had now been resolved. After the French had rejected the European

Defense Community in 1954, the British had come up with an expanded Western European Union which made possible the arming of Germany with its forces incorporated into NATO and Western recognition of the sovereignty of West Germany. The Russians had responded in early 1955 by creating the Warsaw Pact, a military alliance consisting of the Soviet Union, East Germany, and the Eastern European satellites. With the postwar division of Europe complete, public opinion on the continent now called for a negotiated settlement with the Russians to reduce tension. Anthony Eden, who replaced Winston Churchill as England's Prime Minister in early 1955, spoke out strongly for a meeting with the Russians. Dulles still objected, but Eisenhower began to weaken. The President grew tired of the constant questioning of American opposition to a high-level meeting and finally told the press that he was ready to "pick up and go from any place to Timbuktu to the North Pole to do something about this question of peace."[14]

The Russians took two steps to ensure that the conference would take place. The first was an announcement in April that they were now ready to reach an agreement on a peace treaty for Austria, a development they had blocked for nine years. A treaty creating a neutral Austria was quickly signed in May. Then that same month the Soviet delegate to the UN disarmament subcommittee in London suddenly offered a comprehensive plan to control the arms race. Departing from past Russian policy, which had insisted on the abolition of nuclear weapons as the first step toward disarmament, the Soviets now came close to previous Western plans by proposing a sharp reduction in conventional forces and a willingness to accept some form of inspection. There were, to be sure, loopholes in the

Soviet offer, notably the restriction of international monitors to fixed inspection posts "at large ports, at railway junctions, on main motor highways and in aerodromes."[15] But for the first time since disarmament talks had begun in 1946, the Russians were at least willing to discuss the Western concept of international control and supervision.

President Eisenhower approached the forthcoming summit, now scheduled for mid-July in Geneva, with his usual caution. He wrote to a friend that he did not expect any spectacular results from the meeting, but hoped to find out if the Russians were willing to make "a tactical change that could mean, for the next few years at least, some real easing of tension." As time for the conference drew nearer, he began to become more enthusiastic. He realized that there was no likelihood for an agreement on the German issue, but, according to Sherman Adams, he hoped "to make the meeting a solid beginning of a move toward world disarmament."[16]

The President's concern for controlling the arms race dominated his preparations for the Geneva Conference. In March he had appointed Harold Stassen as his special assistant on disarmament, charging him with the difficult task of reconciling differences between various branches of the government and using his dogged perseverance to arrive at a consensus in this area. Surprised by the May Soviet disarmament proposal, Eisenhower then asked another presidential assistant, Nelson Rockefeller, who had succeeded C. D. Jackson in directing Cold War strategy, to develop a new American initiative in the arms field. Rockefeller organized a panel of experts at the Quantico Marine Corps base in Virginia and came up with the idea of mutual aerial inspection. Ike was immediately attracted to this new approach, but when Dulles raised objections, he agreed to await developments at the Geneva Conference before deciding whether or not to present it to the Russians. Thus the President ordered Rockefeller and Stassen to stand by in Paris when the conference opened and be ready to join him in Geneva with the new proposal.

The President's natural optimism burst forth when he left for the summit meeting. Disregarding Dulles's advice not to lift the hopes of the American people too high, Eisenhower gave a nation-wide television and radio address in which he said that he was going to Geneva "to change the spirit that has characterized the intergovernmental relationships of the world during the past ten years." In his opening address to the conference, he stressed the same theme. Admitting that the assembled leaders could not expect to solve all the world's problems, he nevertheless expressed the determination "to find a basis for accommodation which will make life safer and happier. . . ." Above all, he wanted to "create a new spirit that will make possible future solutions. . . ."[17]

The first few days at Geneva proved disappointing. Even though the conference was only designed to explore and open up problems to be discussed in detail at a subsequent meeting of the foreign ministers, the heads of government made little progress. The Soviet leaders, Marshal Bulganin, who held the title of Premier, and Nikita Khrushchev, who wielded the real power, were unyielding in the formal sessions and only slightly less rigid in the more casual social encounters. "They drank little and smiled much," Eisenhower commented, but he soon realized that "their efforts to ingratiate" were "obviously planned and rehearsed."

After several days of fruitless discussion on the German issue, the President decided to take a gamble. He ordered

Harold Stassen and Nelson Rockefeller to join him in Geneva and conferred with them for several hours on the details of the aerial inspection plan. After showing it to Anthony Eden, who immediately approved, the President decided to go ahead with what became known as "open skies," though he was still not sure whether to include it in his formal presentation on disarmament or to save it for later in the conference.[18]

The next day, acting on impulse, Eisenhower took off his glasses and began speaking directly to the Soviet leaders as he laid out the open skies concept. The United States, he said, was prepared to exchange military blueprints of all its armed forces for those of the Soviet Union and to permit regular and frequent aerial inspection of its territory in return for similar privileges on the part of the Russians. Speaking mainly from memory, the President concluded his presentation with an earnest appeal: "I do not know how I could convince you of our sincerity in this matter and that we mean you no harm. I only wish that God would give me some means of convincing you of our sincerity and loyalty in making this proposal." As if on cue, a late afternoon thunderstorm broke with a flash of lightning and the lights suddenly went out in the conference room, plunging the gathering into a few seconds of total darkness.[19]

The British and French leaders quickly voiced their approval of open skies; the Russians, obviously caught by surprise, withheld any immediate reaction. Bulganin promised only to give it careful study, but when Eisenhower told him, "The United States will never take part in an aggressive war," the Soviet Premier immediately responded, "We believe that statement." Khrushchev, however, came up to Eisenhower during cocktails at the end of that day's session and said ominously, "I don't agree with the chairman." According to Ambassador Bohlen, who translated Khrushchev's remarks, the Soviet leader went on to ask Eisenhower "whom he was trying to fool?" "In our eyes," Khrushchev continued, "this is a very transparent espionage device. . . . You could hardly expect us to take this seriously." The Russians never formally rejected open skies, but by their inaction, as Bohlen noted, they let it "die of malnutrition."[20]

Most observers have agreed with Khrushchev's evaluation of open skies. Peter Lyon called it "a spectacular victory for the Cold Warriors" who practiced psychological warfare. He noted that in discussing the idea with Rockefeller and Stassen, Eisenhower observed that since the Russians already knew the location of most American military bases, "mutual agreements for such overflights would undoubtedly benefit us more than the Russians, because we know very little about their installations." Historian Herbert Parmet agreed, calling the proposal "a grand gesture" and citing the President's remark to an interviewer in 1965: "We knew the Soviets wouldn't accept it. We were sure of that." Yet while it is true that open skies clearly benefited the United States, it is unlikely that Eisenhower was sure it would be rejected. His 1965 remarks reflect rather the desire to take the sting out of the Soviet rebuff. Bernhard Bechhoefer is right in pointing out that Eisenhower, both in atoms-for-peace and open skies, was breaking away from the previous Western insistence on comprehensive disarmament proposals and searching instead for more limited measures that could break the deadlock and help bring the arms race under some measure of control. Eisenhower offered open skies as "a system . . . to develop the mutual confidence which will open wide the avenues of progress for all our peoples." In a letter to General Alfred Gruenther on July 25, the President described his proposal at Geneva as a way to achieve "an immense gain in mutual confidence and trust." Seen in this light, rather than as a cynical Cold War ploy, open skies stands as a flawed but sincere attempt by Eisenhower to reduce international tension.[21]

The Geneva Conference failed to achieve the détente that some hoped for. The leaders resolved neither the problem of Germany nor the disarmament stalemate, and the subsequent session of the foreign ministers made no headway. The only positive result was an agreement on cultural exchanges and the phrase "spirit of Geneva," an outgrowth of Eisenhower's optimistic expectations. The real significance of the conference was the evident realization by both sides that nuclear war was unthinkable. Emmet Hughes spoke of Geneva as signifying "the acceptance by the major powers of the common necessity to shun recourse to nuclear war." Spokesmen for both sides agreed with that appraisal. Thus Harold Macmillan, the British foreign secretary, claimed that the summit revealed that all the great nations "now accepted that modern war, that is nuclear war, was quite impossible and could only lead to mutual destruction." Four months after the close of the meeting, Nikita Khrushchev expressed the same thought, observing that Geneva had "led to recognition by the Great Powers of the senselessness of war, which in view of the development of atomic and hydrogen weapons, can only bring misfortune to mankind."[22]

This common understanding of the nuclear danger was in itself a valuable development. Equally important was the emergence at Geneva of Dwight Eisenhower as the world's most eloquent spokesman for peace. Commenting

on the impact of Eisenhower's personality—his friendliness
and spontaneity, his warmth and naturalness—Robert
Donovan concluded, "Eisenhower conveyed a sense of de-
cency and dignity which mocked the picture of his country
as an immature nation hell-bent for war." Journalist
Richard Rovere also thought the President had scored an
impressive personal triumph, noting, "The man has an
absolutely unique ability to convince people that he has
no talent for duplicity." Even the skeptical French were
charmed. "Eisenhower, whose personality has long been
misunderstood," commented *Le Monde* of Paris, "has
emerged as the kind of leader that humanity needs to-
day."[23] Thus Eisenhower's transparent sincerity and honest desire for peace now radiated out to the world; the
President had become the nation's single most valuable
asset in the continuing struggle with the Soviet Union.

IV

The hopes raised by the Geneva summit did not last very
long. The brutal Soviet invasion of Hungary and the tension created by the Suez crisis in 1956 plunged the world
back into the depths of the Cold War. This renewed sense
of danger doomed a fresh attempt to break the disarmament deadlock—a ban on nuclear weapons tests. Adlai
Stevenson, the Democratic presidential candidate in 1956,
first made this proposal in the spring, and then raised it
again in the fall campaign. Operating on the assumption
that nuclear tests could be easily detected without on-site
inspection, the Democratic challenger contended that a
test ban would both spare the world the health hazards

from fallout and serve as a first step toward limiting the arms race. Even though the administration had been seriously considering making such a proposal in September, Eisenhower came out strongly against Stevenson's test ban, arguing that such a sensitive issue should not become enmeshed in partisan politics. When the Soviets embarrassed Stevenson by endorsing his test ban publicly, the administration reaffirmed its opposition, asserting that a test ban could only be considered as part of a broader disarmament plan that included the cessation of nuclear weapons production. The American people apparently agreed with the President, as they re-elected him by an impressive margin in the November election.

Despite his defeat, Stevenson had touched on a sensitive public nerve with his test ban proposal. In the spring of 1957, growing worldwide concern over the danger of fallout created a powerful impulse for a halt to atmospheric testing. Albert Schweitzer made an eloquent appeal for an end to weapons testing, while Linus Pauling, a Nobel prize winner in chemistry, secured the signatures of over 9000 scientists calling for a test ban. Hearings held before a subcommittee of the Joint Committee on Atomic Energy highlighted the possibility that even the small amount of radiation from tests in the atmosphere could increase the incidence of cancer and cause unknown genetic damage. The AEC, supported by many independent scientists, challenged these assertions, but the fact that no one could be certain as to the exact effects of nuclear fallout on human health and well-being proved unsettling.[24]

The President shared in the developing concern over the harmful effects of fallout from nuclear testing. In a letter to Representative Sterling Cole of New York in May 1957, Ike explained that the "whole question of testing of atomic weapons has engaged my concern from the time I first took office." He had instructed Lewis Strauss to confine tests "to the absolute minimum," and far from being "inflexible" on this issue, Eisenhower had been engaged in "a constant effort to find a way out of what has for so many years seemed an impasse." When the Russians suddenly proposed a two-to-three-year moratorium on testing under some form of international inspection, the President permitted Harold Stassen to pursue negotiations on a separate test ban with the Russians at the United Nations Disarmament Subcommittee meeting in London in 1957. "I would be perfectly delighted to make some satisfactory arrangement for temporary suspension of tests," Ike told a press conference on June 19.[25]

The possibility of separating out the test ban from a comprehensive disarmament package worried both Secretary of State Dulles and AEC Chairman Lewis Strauss. Dulles tried to restrain Stassen's activities in London while Strauss concentrated on the President. On June 24, 1957, Strauss brought a delegation of scientists led by Ernest O. Lawrence and Edward Teller to persuade the President not to halt the AEC's tests. Lawrence explained that American scientists were on the verge of a breakthrough which would enable them to perfect a "clean" H-bomb— one virtually free of deadly fallout—within six or seven years. A test ban which stopped this promising development would be a "crime against humanity." Eisenhower expressed genuine interest in a "clean" bomb, but at the same time he pointed out the growing pressure of world opinion for a test ban and warned that he could not permit the United States to be "crucified on a cross of atoms." The concept of a clean bomb apparently fascinated the President. At his next press conference, he backed away from his earlier support for a separate test ban agreement and reaffirmed the traditional American view that a test ban would have to be part of a comprehensive treaty which cut off the production of all nuclear weapons. Then he surprised everyone by claiming that the scien-entists had assured him that with continued testing for four or five more years, they expected to produce "an absolutely clean bomb." Most experts doubted that all fallout could be removed from a hydrogen bomb, but for the moment at least, the prospects for a separate test ban had fallen victim to the clean bomb concept.[26]

Negotiations for a moratorium on testing continued through the summer of 1957 at London, as first Stassen and then Dulles presented the American proposal for a two-year suspension linked to a Soviet agreement to a future cut-off in nuclear weapons production. This effort failed in late August when the Russians rejected the final American offer and broke off the negotiations. The dramatic launching of Sputnik, the first earth satellite, in October further dimmed hopes for a test ban agreement. This demonstration of Soviet technological skill led to demands in the United States for a concerted effort to catch up with and surpass the Russians in the field of rockets and missiles. In an effort to reassure a shaken American public, Eisenhower created a new President's Science Advisory Committee, headed by MIT President James Killian, who resigned his academic post to become Eisenhower's full-time science adviser. Killian quickly recruited a number of prominent scientists, many of whom had never before served as governmental consultants; now the President would have a far broader range of technical advisers to offset the rigid views of Strauss, Lawrence, and Teller.

The test ban issue came to a head in 1958. The Soviet Union began a series of huge H-bomb tests in February, while the United States planned an extensive series, code-named HARDTACK, for its Pacific proving grounds in the late spring and summer. By mid-March, the administration had learned that the Soviets might declare a voluntary moratorium on further tests when their series was completed. John Foster Dulles feared that such a move would prove embarrassing to the United States, leading to worldwide demands that America follow the Russian lead and cancel HARDTACK. Harold Stassen had resigned as disarmament adviser in February after the administration had rejected his proposal for a two-year suspension of testing; with his chief rival gone, Dulles began to shift his position toward a test ban. Aware of the growing global outcry over fallout and the effective way in which the Soviets could capitalize on it at the end of their current test series, Dulles was now ready to take the initiative.

President Eisenhower convened a meeting of his top national security advisers at the White House on March 24, 1958. Dulles opened the session by pointing out the likelihood that Khrushchev would attempt to win a great propaganda victory by announcing a unilateral suspension of testing in the next few days at the conclusion of the current Russian series. Such a step, Dulles warned, would place the United States "in an extremely difficult position throughout the world." The Soviets had steadily been outmaneuvering the United States on the peace issue since the Geneva summit; a unilateral Russian test ban would result in "very serious losses to us in respect to our allies and the neutrals." Therefore, Dulles proposed that the President immediately announce an American test suspension to become effective at the end of the HARDTACK series. Representatives of the military and the AEC argued strongly against this proposal, warning that future tests were needed to perfect a variety of important weapons, including warheads for Polaris and other advanced missile systems. The President supported his secretary of state, pointing out that opposition to past Soviet test ban proposals had placed the United States in an awkward position. A test ban might hurt the nation militarily, he conceded, but "we need some basis of hope for our own people and for world opinion." It was simply "intolerable," Ike added, that this country "is unable to achieve an advantageous impact on world opinion." In the face of the adamant opposition from the military, however, Dulles finally withdrew his proposal. The President reluctantly agreed not to make any announcement of American intentions about future tests, but as the meeting ended, he asked his advisers "to think about what could be done to get rid of the terrible impasse in which we now find ourselves with regard to disarmament."[27]

Just as Dulles had predicted, the Soviet announced a unilateral suspension of nuclear testing on March 31, adding that they would have to reconsider their action if the United States continued its own test program. While the Russians reaped an impressive propaganda victory, the administration went ahead with the HARDTACK series. The President, however, now received a significant report from his scientific advisers which opened up new possibilities for a test ban agreement. A panel headed by Hans Bethe of Cornell University reported on March 28 that a network of control posts could detect nuclear explosions as small as 2 kilotons. The full scientific advisory committee met in early April and on the basis of the Bethe panel report recommended that the President "stop testing after the HARDTACK series." Since it was now feasible to create an effective inspection system, the committee concluded that a test ban would serve the national interest. The President concurred, and in late April he instructed Dulles to invite Khrushchev to send a team of Soviet technical experts to seek agreement on an inspection system. Without making any explicit promises, the administration was signaling the Russians its intention of entering into a test ban agreement once the inspection problem had been solved.[28]

Khrushchev quickly accepted the American proposal, and delegations of Soviet and American scientists met for six weeks at Geneva in the summer of 1958. By mid-August they had reached agreement on a worldwide network of 180 control posts which they believed would be capable of detecting all nuclear explosions, whether conducted in the atmosphere or underground, greater than 5 kilotons. Aware of this progress, Eisenhower began to discuss the next step with his advisers—the negotiation of a test ban agreement. Once again the Pentagon objected, but now armed with the support of both Dulles and Killian, the President decided to opt for an end to testing. When John McCone, Lewis Strauss's successor as AEC chairman, voiced the unanimous opposition of the AEC members, Eisenhower replied that "the Commission is not concerned with the question of world political position." ". . . our world situation," the President continued, "requires that we achieve the political benefits of this action."[29] Clearly it was Eisenhower's confidence in his own military judgment and his awareness that he had to take into account the international outcry over fallout that led to his momentous decision.

On August 22, 1958, the President announced that he

had invited the Soviets to attend a conference on October 31 of all nations possessing nuclear weapons to create an international control system and negotiate a test ban treaty. As a sign of good faith, Eisenhower offered to suspend future American testing for one year, provided that the Russians would also refrain from testing during that period. If the negotiations proved successful, the United States was prepared to extend the moratorium for another year. Above all, the President expressed his hope that the test ban negotiations would become a first step toward "more substantial agreements" on nuclear disarmament.

A few days later Khrushchev agreed to enter into the proposed test ban talks, and the two countries now settled on Geneva as the site for the meeting. The Soviets refused to say whether they would join the moratorium on testing after October 31, and for the next two months both the United States and the Soviet Union engaged in a last-minute orgy of nuclear detonations—the AEC conducted nineteen tests while the Russians held fourteen. When the conference opened at Geneva on October 31, Khrushchev had not yet agreed to the voluntary moratorium. The United States detected Russian tests on November 1 and 3, but these were apparently the last in the fall Russian series. For the next three years, there were no additional nuclear tests, to the great relief of those who worried over the effect of fallout on human health. Eisenhower had scored a significant diplomatic victory by taking the initiative in halting nuclear tests in the atmosphere, and thus winning worldwide approval. At the same time, he had done what he had always opposed, agreed to stop testing without a functioning inspection system and without any corresponding Soviet concessions on halting nuclear weapons production. In the minds of his military advisers, he had taken a dangerous gamble with American security; Eisenhower, however, was convinced that he had assumed an acceptable risk in the cause of peace. Less concerned with fallout than with the nuclear arms race itself, he hoped that a test ban treaty would be the first step toward a comprehensive disarmament agreement.[30]

V

The optimism created by the moratorium on testing and the opening of the Geneva negotiations did not last very long. On November 10, 1958, Nikita Khrushchev renewed the Berlin crisis, quiet since the end of the blockade in 1949, by announcing Soviet intentions of signing a separate peace treaty with East Germany. Such a move would leave the Western-occupied portions of Berlin isolated 110-miles deep within a Communist nation and call into question the occupation rights of the United States and its allies. On November 27 the new Berlin crisis took on ominous proportions when the Russians sent the Western nations a note declaring their intention of signing the feared peace treaty with East Germany within six months if a negotiated solution to the Berlin problem could not be reached. The only concession Khrushchev offered was to make West Berlin into a free city, provided that it was demilitarized and separated politically from West Germany. The seriousness of the situation was underlined by a Soviet warning that the West should not resort to "threats of force." ". . . only madmen can go to the length of unleashing another world war over the preservation of privileges of occupiers in West Berlin," the Russian note concluded.[31]

Neither contemporary observers nor later analysts were sure exactly what Khrushchev had in mind in issuing the six-month ultimatum. Some believed that he was acting aggressively, trying to split apart the NATO allies. The Soviet success with Sputnik and the growing fears that the Russians were opening up a dangerous missile gap suggested that Khrushchev was intent on securing the maximum advantage from the apparent shift in the military balance of power. Others saw the Russian leader as operating out of a deep-seated fear of a rearmed Germany. The United States had secured NATO agreement to place American nuclear-tipped intermediate-range ballistic missiles (IRBMs) in European sites, and though no IRBMs were yet stationed in Germany, American forces there were known to be equipped with tactical nuclear weapons. The West had steadily refused to recognize East Germany, and had instead insisted on free elections and the reunification of Germany. By using the Berlin situation to force the United States and its allies to accept the permanent division of Germany, Khrushchev could achieve a major aim of Soviet foreign policy and remove for all time the Russian nightmare of a united Germany aligned with the West and armed with nuclear weapons. At the same time, by isolating West Berlin as a free city, Khrushchev could halt the constant flow of refugees from East Germany. Since 1949, nearly three million had fled through Berlin, draining East Germany of its most productive and best trained young people.[32]

Whatever Khrushchev's motivation, the Soviet ultimatum, with its May 27 deadline, posed a difficult dilemma for the Eisenhower administration. The United States lacked the conventional military strength to defend its position in Berlin. There were only 10,000 troops in the city and less than two understrength Army corps in all Europe; the President estimated that it would take three or four Army corps, each consisting of three or four divisions, to seize and hold an access route into Berlin. A nuclear threat seemed equally empty. The Soviets not only possessed H-bombs to match those of the United States, but they had enough IRBMs to wipe out Western Europe. And even the diplomatic outlook appeared bleak. The NATO allies could not agree on German policy. Charles de Gaulle, who had returned to power in France, had little enthusiasm for the idea of German reunification, though he did think that the West should stand firm on Berlin. The British prime minister, Harold Macmillan, reflected the growing realization of his people that England would be a prime target for Soviet nuclear retaliation. Accordingly, Macmillan was eager to enter into negotiations, possibly at a summit conference, and explore the idea of making West Berlin into a free city.

Eisenhower was determined to stand fast on Berlin, despite the military weakness of the Western position. In a statement at a NATO meeting in December 1957, the President had expressed his basic view on Berlin by saying, "Any sign of Western weakness at this forward position could be misinterpreted with grievous consequences." Khrushchev's ultimatum did not shake his resolve. He felt the United States had a "solemn obligation," he stated in his memoirs, to defend the two million citizens of West Berlin. At the same time, he recognized the difficulty of taking any effective action. After a conference with his principal national security advisers on December 11, he resisted any talk of using force to defend Berlin. He favored a diplomatic solution, and finally instructed Dulles to work out a joint reply to the Russian note on Berlin with the NATO allies. He wanted the Western response to "make it plain that the U.S. does not want war." "But if they deny us our rights," the President added, "then we'll have to reassess our position. They've got to know that we're willing to put our whole stack in the pot."[33]

In late December, the Western nations sent identical replies to the Russian note of November 27. They rejected the six-month ultimatum, reaffirmed Western rights in Berlin based on the occupation agreements at the end of World War II, and yet expressed a willingness to negotiate not only on Berlin but on the broader issue of an overall German settlement. The Russians indicated they were ready to enter into such negotiations, but they refused to lift the May 27 deadline.

The President now had to face the question of how the United States would respond if the Russians went ahead and signed a separate peace treaty with East Germany. At a White House meeting on January 28, 1959, General Nathan Twining, chairman of the Joint Chiefs of Staff, recommended that the United States should be prepared to send in an Army division to secure access to Berlin if the East Germans halted American truck convoys. Secretary of State Dulles immediately objected, warning that world opinion would not support such an aggressive move. Twining responded by saying that any smaller use of force would be easily repulsed, forcing the United States to back down. He was ready, he asserted, "to fight a general nuclear war."

Eisenhower intervened at this point to side with his secretary of state. One division, he contended, would be too large for a show of force but at the same time "lacked capability" to open up full access to Berlin across 110 miles of enemy territory. In such a delicate situation, he preferred to "give peace forces a chance." He then said that if the East Germans stopped an American vehicle after May 27, the United States would try to send a small armed convoy to Berlin. If this probe was halted, then Eisenhower would order an airlift, break off relations with the Soviet Union, take the whole issue to the United Nations, and prepare for general war. The President thus made clear his ultimate determination to defend Berlin while at the same time refusing to be stampeded into an overly aggressive response. In the last analysis, he was prepared to risk nuclear war over Berlin, but not before every other possibility had been exhausted. "Our approach was cautious, controlled," Eisenhower commented later, "and I was confident that it was correct."[34]

While the crisis continued to mount, the American people got a glimpse of Eisenhower's policy in his press conference replies to reporters' questions. He ruled out the use of conventional weapons, telling reporters that the United States had no plans "to shoot our way into Berlin" and asserting that "we are certainly not going to fight a ground war in Europe." At the same time, when a reporter asked him if the United States was ready "to use nuclear weapons if necessary to defend free Berlin," Ike replied, "Well, I don't know how you could free anything with nuclear weapons." But then he went on to say that the United States was prepared to meet its "responsibilities with respect to Berlin." Any movement toward "real hostilities," he added, would have to come "from the side of the Soviets." Only then would he make his final response. Thus the President took refuge in ambiguity, just as he had during the Formosa Straits crisis. Aware of the tactical situation in Berlin, he ruled out a ground war, but he left open the possibility of a nuclear conflict, always with the understanding that he would never fire the first shot. Walking a careful line between firmness and conciliation, Eisenhower sought to convince the Russians that the best answer to the Berlin crisis lay in diplomacy, not war.[35]

The tension began to break in March. Harold Macmillan journeyed to Russia and came back with word that Khrushchev was willing to call off the May 27 deadline in return for Western agreement for a new summit conference. Macmillan came to the United States in late March to urge Eisenhower to grant this Soviet condition. The President expressed his reluctance to attend a summit conference unless there was substantial progress toward a settlement at a lower level. When Macmillan pleaded with the President, expressing his belief that as few as eight nuclear missiles could wipe out England, Ike finally agreed to a foreign ministers conference with the Soviets, with a summit meeting in the future "as soon as developments justify." Khrushchev quickly accepted this formula, and, while the Russians never formally gave up their May 27 deadline, the agreement to meet at the foreign ministers level in Geneva on May 11 effectively removed the ultimatum.[36]

John Foster Dulles was not able to represent the United States at Geneva. Stricken by a recurrence of the abdominal cancer that he had first suffered during the Suez crisis, Dulles resigned as secretary of state in mid-April. Eisenhower replaced him with Christian Herter, who had served as undersecretary of state for the past year. Herter was experienced in foreign policy, but he lacked the national stature and the rapport with Eisenhower that had been Dulles's strength. Although the new secretary of state represented the United States ably at the Geneva Conference, Soviet intransigence prevented any headway.

The diplomats adjourned their negotiations to fly to Washington to attend the funeral of John Foster Dulles on May 27, ironically the day the earlier Soviet ultimatum expired.

The deadlock at Geneva convinced Eisenhower that a summit conference would be useless, but the British continued to push hard for the meeting. The President finally agreed to an intermediate step. Persuaded by Herter and Robert Murphy, the new undersecretary of state and Ike's old wartime diplomatic adviser, Eisenhower issued an invitation to Nikita Khrushchev to visit the United States and meet privately with the President following his tour of the country. Murphy, who passed on this offer to a high-level Soviet official visiting the United States, misunderstood Ike's instructions and failed to condition the invitation on progress at the deadlocked Geneva Conference. Eisenhower was furious when Khrushchev accepted without offering any concessions at the foreign ministers meeting, which finally recessed in mid-August without accomplishing anything.

As the time for Khrushchev's visit neared, Eisenhower began to view it as a good opportunity to use his personal charm. ". . . any President that refused finally to use the last atom of prestige" in the cause of peace, Ike told a press conference on August 25, "ought to be condemned by the American people." Privately he planned to use the meeting "for one great personal effort, before leaving office, to soften up the Soviet leader even a little bit." When Khrushchev arrived in Washington, he raised Ike's hopes by stating his belief that the President did not want war and adding, "we assume that you also believe this about us." Eisenhower responded by telling Khrushchev that he had the chance "to go down in history as one of the truly great statesmen of all time" if he would help the President end the Cold War.[37]

Khrushchev undertook a ten-day whirlwind tour of the nation and then went to Camp David for a face-to-face meeting with Eisenhower. The Soviet leader repeated his desire for a summit conference, while Ike made clear his refusal to negotiate while under the threat of a separate peace treaty with East Germany. After several days of discussion, the two men finally agreed on a formula. Eisenhower would drop his demand for substantial progress on a lower level and attend a summit in the spring of 1960; Khrushchev would remove any time limit on the negotiations and withdraw his plan for a Soviet-East German peace treaty. There was no agreement on a Berlin settlement and no progress toward one; the two leaders had simply agreed to continue negotiating.

Despite the lack of accomplishment, the Camp David meeting did help to defuse the tense Berlin crisis. In a press conference the day after Khrushchev left the United States, Eisenhower announced that the Soviet leader had removed the element of duress by agreeing that, while the negotiations "should not be prolonged indefinitely," neither could there be a "fixed time limit on them." The President expressed satisfaction that with the end of the threat of a separate East German treaty, all element of compulsion had been removed from the negotiations. At the same time, he startled American observers by agreeing with Khrushchev's description of the Berlin situation as "abnormal" and indicated a willingness to seek a more enduring solution. The next day, back in Moscow, Khrushchev confirmed Eisenhower's statement that he had agreed that there should be no time limit on the Berlin negotiations, but the Soviet leader also stressed his intention of settling the question of West Berlin "without delay."[38]

In his memoirs, Eisenhower claimed that as a result of his diplomacy at Camp David "a crisis over Berlin had been averted without the surrender of any Western rights." Yet in fact Khrushchev had persuaded the President to agree to a summit conference without any adequate assurance of prior progress toward a settlement in return for lifting a time limit that the Soviet leader had arbitrarily imposed in the first place. Nevertheless, Eisenhower was right in feeling that his diplomacy had been effective. The military situation in Berlin placed the United States in a very perilous position; the longer the President could postpone a showdown, the better the chance for avoiding a nuclear confrontation. Eisenhower's combination of firmness and restraint had clearly impressed Khrushchev, who realized that the President wanted a peaceful solution but could not be sure how the United States would respond to direct Soviet provocation. The American people, sensing the prudent way in which Eisenhower had averted a showdown over Berlin, responded by giving him a strong vote of confidence, as reflected in the Gallup poll, where his popularity rose from a post-Sputnik low of 49 per cent to a respectable 66 per cent in November 1959. The "spirit of Camp David" may have been no more substantial than the afterglow of the Geneva summit in 1955, but everyone breathed a little easier when the President opted for diplomacy rather than force over Berlin.[39]

VI

Two items headed the agenda for the 1960 summit conference, scheduled to be held in Paris in May. The first was Berlin, with the outlook for a negotiated settlement bleak. The second was a comprehensive test ban treaty, and here the prospect was brighter. After nearly two years of negotiation, and several setbacks, the Geneva test ban talks finally seemed to be on the verge of a significant breakthrough.

The conference that had begun on October 31, 1958, quickly bogged down on the issue of on-site inspection. The Russians, fearful as always of foreign probing of their society, wanted to restrict the control system to fixed posts; the United States insisted on the inclusion of inspection teams authorized to make spot checks on suspicious events. Everyone agreed that instruments alone would be sufficient to detect any atmospheric nuclear explosions. The problem arose over underground tests, since it was very difficult to distinguish between an earthquake and a subsurface blast on a seismograph. The diplomats at Geneva soon became deadlocked over this issue, with the Russians stubbornly resisting the American demand for on-site privileges.

New data produced by underground shots in the 1958 HARDTACK test series complicated the problem even more. On January 5, 1959, the United States announced that underground tests were much more difficult to detect than had previously been suspected. Thus the Geneva control system, with its projected 180 monitoring stations, could verify explosions above 20 kilotons in size and not those down to 5 kilotons, as the experts had originally thought possible. Eisenhower found it very embarrassing to make this announcement to the Russians, and he was furious with his scientific advisers for putting him into such a difficult position. "If such discoveries could bring about drastic changes in the structure of fact upon which we made our calculations," he pointed out, "what new discoveries were in the offing?" By March, Edward Teller and Albert Latter of the Rand Corporation had calculated that the detonation of an underground blast in a large cavern could muffle the resulting explosion's seismic waves by a factor of 300. Decoupling, as the new concept was called, would make it theoretically possible to test a nuclear weapon as large as 1 megaton with a resulting seismic signal smaller than that from a normal 5 kiloton blast.[40]

With a comprehensive test ban now in doubt, Eisenhower turned to a more modest proposal—a ban on nuclear explosions in the atmosphere. Several American senators had already made this suggestion, pointing out that scientists were agreed that they could detect atmospheric blasts quite easily at long distances. Such a limited test ban would not halt the arms race, since the United States and Russia could continue to perfect new weapons through underground tests. But it would relieve the worldwide concern over fallout, a fear that had been intensified in the spring of 1959 by the heavy radioactivity caused by the extensive Soviet and American tests that had preceded the 1958 moratorium. Accordingly, at a meeting with Harold Macmillan at Camp David in March 1959, the President agreed to offer the Russians a ban limited to atmospheric tests "at least for three or four years." The British Prime Minister gave his approval, and Eisenhower, though disappointed at the conditional nature of the offer, felt relieved. ". . . in the long run," he commented, "there is nothing but war—if we give up all hope of a peaceful solution."

The President offered the atmospheric test ban to Khrushchev in a letter on April 13, 1959. Reiterating his desire for a comprehensive agreement, Eisenhower put forth the limited test ban as an interim measure designed to spare the world any "additions to levels of radioactivity" while the negotiators continued to search for a way to stop all nuclear experiments. The atmospheric test ban, he pointed out, would not require any on-site inspection, and the control system to monitor it could be quite simple, with only a few posts on Russian soil. The Soviets, however, were not receptive. Their chief negotiator at Geneva dismissed it as meaningless; a week later, Khrushchev rejected it as "misleading," saying that it would give the public a false assurance while failing to halt the nuclear arms race. Then, adopting an idea suggested earlier by Macmillan, the Soviet leader offered to break the deadlock over on-site inspection by setting an annual quota for such activity. "Of course," Khrushchev added, "the number of annual trips by inspection teams should not be great."

Eisenhower was disappointed at the Soviet rejection of his atmospheric test ban offer. His advisers, moreover, were skeptical of the quota proposal for on-site inspection. Killian warned that there were between 1000 and 1500 earthquakes a year in Russia that would have to be checked out; the military doubted that an agreement could be reached on an acceptable number of on-site visits. The President, however, was unwilling to follow this pessimistic advice. He spoke of the public's alarm over fallout and the danger of being forced by popular opinion into accepting "worse agreements than what may possibly be available to us in Geneva." Any arrangement carried with it an element of risk, he continued; "one cannot have full certainty." Therefore, he ordered the American negotiators at Geneva to continue to work for a comprehensive test ban treaty and explore the Russian proposal for a quota of on-site inspections. He explained his views to the American people at a press conference in June 1959, saying that there was no foolproof solution to the problem of nuclear testing. "What we do have to do," he contended, "is to refine the process to the point where we minimize risks and indeed bring them down below the level where they could be truly dangerous to our country."[41]

There was no further progress at Geneva in 1959. With the moratorium on testing due to expire on October 31, the President extended it until the end of the year. Then in December, angered by continued Soviet intransigence at Geneva but sensitive to the public's fear of fallout, Eisenhower announced the end of the moratorium, adding that after December 31, 1959, the United States would not resume nuclear testing without advance notice. Khrushchev soon pledged that the Soviet Union would not begin testing again unless the Western nations did so first. But despite the informal continuation of the moratorium on a day-to-day basis, the Geneva talks remained deadlocked over the issue of on-site inspection.

George Kistiakowsky, the President's new science adviser who had replaced Killian in mid-1959, came up with a formula to break the stalemate in early 1960. His threshold concept broadened Eisenhower's earlier atmospheric test ban to include all large underground tests, defined as those that registered 4.75 or more on the Richter seismic scale. Eisenhower revealed the new proposal in a press conference on February 11, 1960, claiming that it provided for "the ending of nuclear weapons tests in all the environments that can now be effectively controlled." The 4.75 Richter threshold would include all underground tests above 20 kilotons, as well as all atmospheric and underwater blasts. At Geneva, American negotiators told the Russians that the United States would be willing to accept a fixed quota of on-site inspections to differentiate between earthquakes and subsurface blasts. The initial Soviet reaction, however, was negative. The chief Soviet negotiator told the press that the only acceptable solution was "a plan to end all tests."[42]

A month later, the Russians reversed themselves and indicated their willingness to accept the threshold plan. There was one condition—the United States would have to agree to a voluntary moratorium on testing below the proposed 4.75 treaty limit. The Russian offer split Eisenhower's advisers. The hard-liners, led by AEC Chairman John McCone, maintained that the Russian plan was unacceptable—they were asking the United States to abandon its traditional insistence on inspection and to accept Russian good faith for the ban on small underground tests. The State Department, with some surprising support from the Pentagon, argued for acceptance of the Soviet proposal, on condition that the moratorium on small underground tests be limited to one or two years. Harold Macmillan, alarmed by criticism of the Soviet proposal in Congress and in the press, telephoned Eisenhower and persuaded the reluctant President to invite him to Washington to discuss the test ban impasse.

The President decided to resolve the issue before the British leader arrived. On March 24, 1960, he met with his principal national security advisers and informed them that he intended to accept the Soviet proposal, with the moratorium limited to one year, or two at the most. John

McCone immediately voiced his suspicion that the Russians would use the moratorium to conduct secret undergrounds tests. Eisenhower replied that he did not see "how the moratorium provision can hurt us," pointing out that American insistence on on-site inspection would make it too risky for the Russians to cheat. When McCone called the proposal "a surrender of our basic policy," Eisenhower "got obviously angry," to the delight of Kistiakowsky. "The President said that he had decided to offer one or two years' test moratorium on executive basis," Kistiakowsky recorded in his diary, "that he didn't think that the Soviets would accept it, but felt that this was in the interest of the country, as otherwise all hope of relaxing the cold war would be gone." The official minutes of this crucial White House meeting record Eisenhower as saying that "he recognized the risks in what we are doing, but pointed out that we have great risks now simply because we are in a cold war."[43]

Harold Macmillan was pleased to discover that the President had already decided to accept the new Russian proposal. The two men spent several days at Camp David spelling out the details of the Western position. The proposed treaty would call for a ban on all nuclear tests in the atmosphere and underground blasts that measured above 4.75 on the Richter scale, a moratorium on underground tests below the 4.75 threshold for one or two years (Macmillan had pushed unsuccessfully for three years), and a fixed number of on-site inspections each year. The negotiators at Geneva could work out most of the details, but two matters would require agreement at the summit—the length of the moratorium and the annual quota of on-site inspections. The last item was the most delicate of all. Eisenhower's advisers wanted at least 100; Macmillan would be willing to settle for 10, but he feared Khrushchev would not agree to more than 5 a year. The final number would have to await the give-and-take of Eisenhower and Khrushchev at the summit.

"All the omens were good," Macmillan wrote in his diary. The British leader was especially impressed by Eisenhower's new enthusiasm for a comprehensive test ban treaty. "He is really keen on this and—although he has not said much about it yet—would accept further concessions in the course of negotiations to get it. . . ." The President shared his optimism with the press. When a reporter asked him if the voluntary moratorium did not represent a gamble, Eisenhower replied, "you have to make some concessions as to stopping this whole business." It was this larger consideration—the halting of the nuclear arms race—that concerned the President the most. "There are already four nations into it, and it's an expensive business," he maintained. "And it could be finally more dangerous than ever. . . ." The risk inherent in the voluntary moratorium seemed slight when weighed against this opportunity for moving toward nuclear disarmament. Atoms-for-peace and open skies had failed to check the momentum of the arms race; now, on the eve of the Paris summit, Ike was ready to negotiate a comprehensive test ban treaty which would be a significant first step toward bringing the runaway arms race under control.[44]

VII

As the time approached for the summit conference, the chances for a genuine breakthrough in the Cold War were mixed. The growing optimism over a test ban treaty had to be balanced against the lack of progress toward a Berlin settlement. Khrushchev's rhetoric on the German issue had been getting tougher in the spring of 1960. He renewed his threat to sign a separate peace treaty with East Germany, asserting that such a step would automatically terminate all Western occupation rights in Berlin. He was careful, however, not to set a time limit for this development. On April 20, Undersecretary of State C. Douglas Dillon replied for the United States. Terming the continued partition of Germany a "monstrous" abnormality, Dillion warned the Soviets that the United States would "not negotiate under duress." "No nation," he asserted, "could preserve its faith in collective security if we permitted the courageous people of West Berlin to be sold into slavery." Several days later, the President endorsed Dillon's remarks, telling the press that "we are not going to give up the juridical rights that we have."[45]

The ill-fated U-2 flight of Francis Gary Powers on May 1, 1960, doomed the summit conference before it ever began. The high altitude intelligence overflights of the Soviet Union had begun in mid-1956, the outgrowth of recommendations of a scientific panel headed by James Killian. The Russians were aware of the flights from the outset, tracking the American spy planes with radar. The high altitude at which the U-2 flew placed the planes beyond the range of both Soviet interceptors and surface-to-air missiles. The photographs taken on these flights gave the United States vital information about Soviet military progress, especially in regard to missiles, but Eisenhower had frequently expressed his reservations about them. "Some day one of these machines is going to be caught," he later recalled having told his advisers, "and we're going to have a storm." About six months before the Paris summit, he suggested at a National Security Council meeting that the flights be halted, but when CIA and State and Defense Department officials all objected, he grudgingly permitted the program to continue. He personally approved two final missions before the summit, one on April 9 which brought back indications that the Russians were building their first operational ICBM base east of the Urals, and a second, scheduled for April 30, designed to follow up on this potentially crucial information. When bad weather forced cancellation of the April 30th flight, Eisenhower gave permission to conduct it on May 1, just fifteen days before the summit conference was due to begin in Paris.

An aide informed the President on the afternoon of May 1 that Powers's plane was overdue and presumed missing. The next day the CIA confirmed that the plane had been lost; Eisenhower, who had been assured that the U-2 was equipped to self-destruct in an emergency, assumed that no evidence would survive to link the plane with the United States. The National Aeronautical and Space Administration released a long-standing cover story to the effect that an American weather plane had accidentally strayed into Russian territory and was missing. When Khrushchev announced to the world on May 5 that the Soviets had shot down an American spy plane, Eisenhower was concerned, but he permitted the State Department to confirm the original NASA statement and suggest that the so-called spy plane was in fact a peaceful weather research aircraft that had simply lost its way.[46]

On May 8, Khrushchev stunned the Eisenhower administration and shocked the world by announcing that the Soviet Union had not only shot down the U-2 but captured the pilot alive and the wreckage of his plane intact. While gloating over this revelation, Khrushchev still left Eisenhower with a graceful way out. "I am prepared to grant that the President had no knowledge of a plane being dispatched to the Soviet Union," the Russian leader declared, blaming the flight on "militarists" in America who "begin to run the show." Ike was now in a quandary. Given the fact of Powers's capture, there was no longer any way to deny the actual flight. If he accepted the convenient out that Khrushchev offered, he would seemingly confirm the idea held by many contemporaries that he was a lazy, incompetent President who delegated his authority to others. On the other hand, to come out openly and take responsibility for the U-2 flight would be unprecedented in the history of espionage and would clearly endanger the upcoming summit conference. Several advisers, accordingly, suggested that the President simply refuse to comment on the whole matter.

At a National Security Council meeting on May 9, Eisenhower announced that he would assume full responsibility for the U-2 mission. "We're going to take a beating on this," he admitted, "And I'm the one, rightly, who is going to have to take the brunt." Later that day Secretary of State Herter issued a new statement confirming that the U-2 flight was an American espionage mission and justifying it on the grounds of protecting the United States against a possible Soviet sneak attack. On May 11, the President told his weekly press conference that "no one wants another Pearl Harbor." Accordingly, he had instructed his subordinates to "gather, in every feasible way, the information required to protect the United States and the free world against surprise attack." In defending the U-2 flights as vital to American security, both the secretary of state and the President implied that the flights would continue in the future.[47]

The fate of the Paris summit now hung in the balance. In Moscow, Khrushchev began to suggest that he could not sit down and negotiate with a man who had deliberately violated Soviet air space. At the very least, it seemed appropriate for Eisenhower to announce that the flights would not be continued. In fact, the President ordered the U-2 missions stopped before he left for Paris, but he stubbornly refused to make this vital decision public. Instead he planned to reveal it at the opening of the summit as part of a conciliatory speech stressing American desire to negotiate a Berlin settlement and a test ban treaty.

Eisenhower had miscalculated. When he arrived in Paris, he found that Khrushchev was now demanding that the President apologize for the Powers flight, punish those responsible for it, and promise to end all future overflights of the Soviet Union. Instead of being able to announce the halting of the U-2 flights as a peaceful gesture, Eisenhower would now appear to be giving in to Khrushchev's demands. Meeting privately on the eve of the opening session with Macmillan and de Gaulle, Ike expressed his resentment by saying, "I hope that no one is under the illusion that I am going to crawl on my knees to Khrushchev." De Gaulle quickly commented, "No one is under that illusion."

The next day Khrushchev spoke first at what was to have been the opening session of the summit conference. In biting, belligerent tones he repeated his demand for an apology and a suspension of the flights as a condition for the conference. As a final insult, the Soviet leader withdrew his earlier invitation for Eisenhower to tour Russia in the summer of 1960. The President replied with barely concealed contempt. He would not apologize for his efforts to protect national security, but he assured Khrushchev that he had already ordered an end to the U-2 flights. The United States, he concluded, was ready to negotiate with the Russians, either at the summit or in separate, bilateral talks. Khrushchev replied by walking out of the conference chamber; the summit was over before it ever began.[48]

The break-up of the Paris summit ended any chance for easing Cold War tensions in the last year of Eisenhower's presidency. On his return to Moscow, Khrushchev ruled out any further negotiations over Berlin, saying that he preferred to wait until after the American elections so that he could deal with Eisenhower's successor. The test ban negotiations continued for another three months at Geneva, but without agreement at the top on the length of a moratorium on small underground shots and on the annual quota for on-site inspections, there was no hope for a treaty. The talks finally adjourned in August; nearly two years of diplomacy had failed to break the impasse at Geneva.

Eisenhower had difficulty coming to terms with the U-2 fiasco and the abortive Paris summit. In a National Security Council meeting on May 24, he ruefully described the Powers mission as a "failure" that happened "at the wrong time." But he would not admit that the administration's conflicting statements about the episode were "errors," and he became furious when an aide spoke of the need to "regain our leadership." Kistiakowsky recorded the President as saying that "we did not lose the leadership and therefore we didn't have to regain it, and he would appreciate it if that expression were never used again." In his memoirs, Ike's only regret was in issuing "a premature and erroneous cover story." He defended the

U-2 program as a "success," claiming that for three-and-a-half years it provided the United States with information on Soviet military deployment that was vital to American national security.[49]

Yet the very stridency of Eisenhower's attempt to justify his handling of the U-2 affair betrays his own sense of failure. He had looked forward to the Paris meeting with much greater optimism than he had the 1955 Geneva Conference; the progress on a nuclear test ban treaty gave genuine promise of a major accomplishment. He revealed the extent of his disappointment in a conversation with George Kistiakowsky in July 1960. ". . . the President began to talk with much feeling," his science adviser recalled, "about how he had concentrated his efforts the last few years on ending the cold war, how he felt that he was making big progress, and how the stupid U-2 mess had ruined all his efforts." Sadly, the President concluded that "he saw nothing worthwhile left for him to do now until the end of his presidency."[50]

VIII

Eisenhower was right. During his last few months in office he was unable to regain the momentum he had been trying to create toward easing Cold War tensions. Instead, he found himself the prisoner of events. In Cuba, the emergence of Fidel Castro led to a growing antagonism and finally a break in diplomatic relations; the sudden grant of independence to the Congo by Belgium caused grave instability in Africa; growing Communist insurgency in South Vietnam and an abortive right-wing coup in Laos created a sense of danger in Southeast Asia that fore-shadowed the tragic Vietnam War of the 1960s. In the fall, the President watched helplessly as Nikita Khrushchev came to the United Nations in New York and attracted worldwide attention by pounding his shoe on the table. His greatest disappointment came in November, when Richard Nixon spurned his help until the climax of the presidential campaign and then lost narrowly to John F. Kennedy, a man Eisenhower felt lacked the experience and maturity to conduct American foreign policy.

The sense of a heightened Cold War troubled Eisen-hower as he left office. His fondest wish had been to use his skills to reduce tension and lessen the possibility of a nu-clear holocaust. His record, however, was far better than the crises of 1960 would suggest. He had halted the Korean War six months after taking office. In the ensuing seven-and-a-half years he had kept the United States at peace. In the Middle East he had managed to contain the Suez crisis and restore temporary stability to that troubled region; in Asia, he had balanced the somewhat flamboyant rhetoric of his secretary of state with his own restraint and achieved a delicate stand-off between the Nationalists and the Chi-nese Communists in the Formosa Straits; in Europe, he had stood fast before Khrushchev's threats over Berlin, maintaining the American commitment to that city while avoiding a resort to force. And if he had failed in his most ambitious undertaking, the control of the arms race, at least he had achieved a cessation of nuclear testing, with its potentially deadly fallout, during the last two years of his term.

The very nature of Eisenhower's presidential style ob-scured his successes and led to the contemporary belief that he was a lazy and ineffective leader. His fondness for indirection robbed him of the credit, as well as the blame, for the actions of the men he let take the limelight, such as John Foster Dulles and Harold Stassen. Yet those close to Eisenhower realized that he alone was making the important decisions and was in full control of his more visible subordinates. Richard Nixon, who as Vice President observed Ike for eight years, once commented, "An Eisenhower characteristic was never to take direct action requiring his personal participation where indirect methods would accomplish the same result."[51] Eisenhower believed that his job was to make the decisions; he left the role of advocacy and debate to others.

The essence of Eisenhower's strength, and the basis for any claim to presidential greatness, lies in his admirable self-restraint. Emmet Hughes had this quality in mind when he wrote: "The man—and the President—was never more decisive than when he held to a steely resolve *not* to do something that he sincerely believed wrong in itself or alien to his office."[52] Nearly all of Eisenhower's foreign policy achievements were negative in nature. He ended the Korean War, he refused to intervene militarily in Indochina, he refrained from involving the United States in the Suez crisis, he avoided war with China over Quemoy and Matsu, he resisted the temptation to force a showdown over Berlin, he stopped exploding nuclear weapons in the atmosphere. A generation of historians and political scientists, bred in the progressive tradition, have applied an activist standard to Ike's negative record and have found it wanting. Yet in the aftermath of Vietnam, it can be argued that a President who avoids hasty military action and refrains from extensive involvement in the internal affairs of other nations deserves praise rather than scorn.

Eisenhower left behind a mixed legacy. His efforts to

liquidate the Cold War and ease the burdens of the arms race failed; he bequeathed to John F. Kennedy situations in Cuba and Vietnam that led to grave crises in the 1960s. But at the same time, his moderation and prudence served as an enduring model of presidential restraint—one that his successors ignored to their eventual regret. Tested by a world as dangerous as any that an American leader has ever faced, Eisenhower used his sound judgment and instinctive common sense to guide the nation safely through the first decade of the thermonuclear age.

Notes

CHAPTER 1: EISENHOWER AND THE PRESIDENCY

1. Cyrus L. Sulzberger, *The Last of the Giants* (New York, 1970), p. 323; Peter Lyon, *Eisenhower: Portrait of the Hero* (Boston, 1974), *passim*.
2. Stephen E. Ambrose, *The Supreme Commander: The War Years of General Dwight D. Eisenhower* (Garden City, N.Y., 1970), p. 325.
3. Harry C. Butcher, *My Three Years With Eisenhower* (New York, 1946), pp. 116, 221, 763.
4. Ambrose, *Supreme Commander*, p. 638.
5. *Ibid.*, p. 97.
6. Kenneth S. Davis, *Soldier of Democracy: A Biography of Dwight D. Eisenhower* (Garden City, N.Y., 1945), p. 548.
7. John Gunther, *Eisenhower: The Man and the Symbol* New York, 1951), p. 87.
8. *Ibid.*, p. 37.
9. Dwight D. Eisenhower, *At Ease: Stories I Tell to Friends* (Garden City, N.Y., 1967), pp. 167–68.
10. John Foster Dulles, "A Policy of Boldness," *Life*, 32 (May 14, 1952), 151.

11. *Ibid.*, pp. 154, 157.
12. Dwight D. Eisenhower, *Mandate for Change, 1953–1956* (Garden City, N.Y., 1963), p. 24.
13. Robert A. Divine, *Foreign Policy and U.S. Presidential Elections, 1952–1960* (New York, 1974), pp. 34–36; C. L. Sulzberger, *Seven Continents and Forty Years* (New York, 1977), p. 144.
14. Divine, *Foreign Policy*, pp. 50–52.
15. Ibid., pp. 52–53.
16. Ibid., pp. 53–54.
17. Ronald J. Caridi, *The Korean War and American Politics: The Republican Party as a Case Study* (Philadelphia, 1968), p. 215.
18. Divine, *Foreign Policy*, pp. 71–72.
19. Ibid., p. 72.
20. Caridi, *Korean War*, pp. 234–35.
21. Sherman Adams, *Firsthand Report* (New York, 1961), p. 44.
22. *Ibid.*, p. 89.
23. Eisenhower, *Mandate for Change*, p. 142. See also Richard H. Immerman, "Eisenhower and Dulles: Who Made the Decisions?", *Political Psychology*, I (Autumn 1979), 3–20.
24. Emmet John Hughes, *The Ordeal of Power* (New York, 1962), pp. 112, 251.
25. *Ibid.*, pp. 252, 264.
26. Lyon, *Eisenhower*, p. 511.
27. Ann Whitman to Marie McCrum, undated, C. D. Jackson Papers, Dwight D. Eisenhower Library, Abilene, Kansas, Box 41.
28. Lyon, *Eisenhower*, pp. 503–4.
29. Robert Cutler, *No Time for Rest* (Boston, 1965), p. 303.
30. Herbert S. Parmet, *Eisenhower and the American Crusades* (New York, 1972), p. 191.
31. Athan G. Theoharis, *The Yalta Myths: An Issue in U.S. Politics, 1945–1955* (Columbus, Mo., 1970), pp. 157–60.
32. Eisenhower, *Mandate*, p. 95.

33. Hughes, *Ordeal*, p. 105.
34. Adams, *Firsthand Report*, p. 98.
35. Quoted in Caridi, *Korean War*, p. 255.
36. Eisenhower, *Mandate*, p. 181.
37. Adams, *Firsthand Report*, p. 48.
38. Mark W. Clark, *From the Danube to the Yalu* (New York, 1954), p. 257.
39. Caridi, *Korean War*, p. 274.

CHAPTER 2: MASSIVE RETALIATION AND ASIA

1. Robert J. Donovan, *Eisenhower: The Inside Story* (New York, 1956), pp. 17–18; Dwight D. Eisenhower, *Mandate for Change, 1953–1956* (Garden City, N.Y., 1963), p. 446.
2. Glenn H. Snyder, "The 'New Look' of 1953," in Warner R. Schilling, Paul Y. Hammond, and Glenn H. Snyder, *Strategy, Politics and Defense Budgets* (New York, 1962), pp. 407–10, 413–15, 422–23, 426–35; Douglas Kinnard, *President Eisenhower and Strategy Management: A Study in Defense Politics* (Lexington, Ky., 1977), p. 27.
3. *The Pentagon Papers*, Senator Gravel Edition (4 vols.; Boston, 1971), I, 416, 426; Snyder, " 'New Look,' " pp. 436–37.
4. Snyder, " 'New Look,' " pp. 451–55, 464.
5. *Public Papers of the Presidents of the United States: Dwight D. Eisenhower, 1954* (Washington, 1960), p. 58; Kinnard, *President Eisenhower*, pp. 140–41, n. 56.
6. *Public Papers of the Presidents: Eisenhower, 1954*, p. 326.
7. *Pentagon Papers*, Gravel edition, I, 407.
8. George Herring, *America's Longest War* (New York, 1979), pp. 25–26.
9. Melvin Gurtov, *The First Vietnam Crisis: Chinese Communist Strategy and United States Involvement, 1953–1954* (New York, 1967), pp. 79–80.

10. *Public Papers of the Presidents: Eisenhower, 1954,* pp. 382–83, 421–22.

11. Herbert S. Parmet, *Eisenhower and the American Crusades* (New York, 1972), p. 358; Eisenhower, *Mandate,* pp. 350–51, 352.

12. Eisenhower, *Mandate,* pp. 340, 352.

13. Donovan, *Eisenhower,* p. 259; Townsend Hoopes, *The Devil and John Foster Dulles* (Boston, 1973), p. 210.

14. *Public Papers of the Presidents: Eisenhower, 1954,* p. 250; Donovan, *Eisenhower,* p. 263; Eisenhower, *Mandate,* p. 345.

15. Eisenhower, *Mandate,* pp. 346–47.

16. *Pentagon Papers,* Gravel edition, I, 461–62, 476; Herring, *America's Longest War,* p. 33.

17. *Ibid.,* p. 35.

18. *Pentagon Papers,* Gravel edition, I, 502–3, 511; Peter Lyon, *Eisenhower: Portrait of the Hero* (Boston, 1974), p. 608.

19. C. L. Sulzberger, *Seven Continents and Forty Years* (New York, 1977), p. 178; Parmet, *Eisenhower,* pp. 367, 368; Alexander Kendrick, *The Wound Within: America in the Vietnam Years, 1945–1974* (Boston, 1974), p. 67.

20. Eisenhower, *Mandate,* p. 341; Parmet, *Eisenhower,* p. 372; Matthew B. Ridgway, *Soldier* (New York, 1956), p. 277; *Pentagon Papers,* Gravel edition, I, 471–72.

21. Walter LaFeber, *America, Russia, and the Cold War, 1945–1975* (3rd ed., New York, 1976), p. 162; Herring, *America's Longest War,* pp. 27, 29–30; Eisenhower, *Mandate,* p. 341; Parmet, *Eisenhower,* p. 377; Gurtov, *First Vietnam Crisis,* p. 136.

22. *Pentagon Papers,* Gravel edition, I, 89, 471.

23. Eisenhower, *Mandate,* p. 354; Hoopes, *Dulles,* p. 230; *Pentagon Papers,* Gravel edition, I, 129n, 512.

24. *Pentagon Papers,* Gravel edition, I, 571.

25. Eisenhower, *Mandate,* p. 372.

26. Herring, *America's Longest War,* pp. 38–39, 42.

27. *The Pentagon Papers,* New York *Times* Edition (New York, 1971), pp. 14–15.

28. Hoopes, *Dulles,* p. 243.

29. Herring, *America's Longest War,* p. 36; Hoopes, *Dulles,* p. 211.

30. Eisenhower, *Mandate,* pp. 460–63; Donovan, *Eisenhower,* p. 301.

31. Eisenhower, *Mandate,* pp. 463–64; Hoopes, *Dulles,* pp. 266–67.

32. John Robinson Beal, *John Foster Dulles* (New York, 1957), p. 227; Eisenhower, *Mandate,* pp. 463, 465–66.

33. Sherman Adams, *Firsthand Report* (New York, 1961), p. 129; James A. Nathan and James K. Oliver, *United States Foreign Policy and World Order* (Boston, 1976), p. 222.

34. Eisenhower, *Mandate,* pp. 466–67; Lyon, *Eisenhower,* p. 635.

35. Hoopes, *Dulles,* pp. 274–75; Donovan, *Eisenhower,* p. 307; Eisenhower, *Mandate,* p. 480.

36. Lyon, *Eisenhower,* pp. 637–38; Beal, *Dulles,* p. 221; Eisenhower, *Mandate,* pp. 471, 472.

37. *Ibid.,* p. 471; Adams, *Firsthand Report,* p. 132.

38. Eisenhower, *Mandate,* pp. 476–77.

39. Hoopes, *Dulles,* pp. 277–78; *Public Papers of the Presidents: Eisenhower, 1955,* p. 332; Eisenhower, *Mandate,* p. 477.

40. Foster Rhea Dulles, *American Foreign Policy Toward Communist China, 1949–1969* (New York, 1972), pp. 155, 157, 159; Lyon, *Eisenhower,* p. 641; Eisenhower, *Mandate,* pp. 478, 481n.

41. *Ibid.,* pp. 478–79; *Public Papers of the Presidents: Eisenhower, 1955,* p. 358.

42. Kenneth T. Young, *Negotiating with the Chinese Communists: The United States Experience, 1953–1967* (New York, 1968), pp. 44, 46.

43. Hoopes, *Dulles,* pp. 277, 281; Lyon, *Eisenhower,* pp. 643, 647.
44. Eisenhower, *Mandate,* p. 483.
45. Dulles, *American Foreign Policy,* p. 175; Dwight D. Eisenhower, *Waging Peace, 1956–1961* (Garden City, N.Y., 1965), pp. 292–94.
46. *Ibid.,* pp. 295–98, 299n.
47. *Ibid.,* p. 299; Hoopes, *Dulles,* pp. 448–49.
48. Harold Macmillan, *Riding the Storm, 1956–1959* (New York, 1971), p. 546; Alexander L. George and Richard Smoke, *Deterrence in American Foreign Policy: Theory and Practice* (New York, 1974), p. 366; Dulles, *American Foreign Policy,* pp. 177, 179; *Public Papers of the Presidents: Eisenhower, 1958,* p. 700.
49. Eisenhower, *Waging Peace,* pp. 302–4.
50. *Ibid.,* p. 295; Macmillan, *Riding the Storm,* p. 555.
51. Hoopes, *Dulles,* p. 449; Eisenhower, *Waging Peace,* p. 295.

CHAPTER 3: EISENHOWER AND THE MIDDLE EAST

1. Robert W. Stookey, *America and the Arab States: An Uneasy Encounter* (New York, 1975), p. 130.
2. *Ibid.,* pp. 63–66; Burton I. Kaufman, "Mideast Multinational Oil, U.S. Foreign Policy, and Antitrust: The 1950s," *Journal of American History,* 63 (March 1977), 952–53.
3. Anthony Sampson, *The Seven Sisters: The Great Oil Companies and the World They Shaped* (New York, 1975), pp. 110–12, 128.
4. Sampson, *Seven Sisters,* p. 117; Richard J. Barnet, *Intervention and Revolution: America's Confrontation with Insurgent Movements Around the World* (Cleveland, 1968), p. 226; Anthony Eden, *Full Circle* (Boston, 1960), p. 214.

5. *Ibid.*, pp. 234–36.
6. *Public Papers of the Presidents: Eisenhower, 1953,* pp. 483–84, 485–86.
7. David Wise and Thomas B. Ross, *The Invisible Government* (New York, 1964), pp. 110–12; Dwight D. Eisenhower, *Mandate for Change, 1953–1956* (Garden City, N.Y., 1963), pp. 164–65; Peter Lyon, *Eisenhower: Portrait of the Hero* (Boston, 1974), pp. 552–53.
8. Eisenhower, *Mandate,* p. 166; John Blair, *The Control of Oil* (New York, 1976), p. 79.
9. Leonard Mosley, *Power Play: Oil in the Middle East* (New York, 1973), pp. 219–20; Sampson, *Seven Sisters,* pp. 129–30; Blair, *Control of Oil,* p. 73.
10. Mosley, *Power Play,* pp. 221–30; Blair, *Control of Oil,* pp. 104–5; Robert Engler, *The Politics of Oil: A Study of Private Power and Democratic Directions* (New York, 1961), pp. 207–9.
11. Eisenhower, *Mandate,* pp. 435, 574; Kaufman, "Mideast Multinational Oil," p. 953.
12. Dwight D. Eisenhower, *Waging Peace, 1956–1961* (Garden City, N.Y., 1965), p. 25. Selwyn Lloyd, *Suez, 1956* (London, 1978), pp. 61–62.
13. Townsend Hoopes, *The Devil and John Foster Dulles* (Boston, 1973), p. 337; Lyon, *Eisenhower,* p. 692; Eisenhower, *Waging Peace,* p. 33.
14. *Ibid.,* p. 34; Engler, *Politics of Oil,* p. 237.
15. Chester Cooper, *The Lion's Last Roar: Suez, 1956* (New York, 1978), p. 119; Eisenhower, *Waging Peace,* pp. 664–65, 667.
16. Hoopes, *Dulles,* pp. 362, 381; Elmo Richardson, *The Presidency of Dwight D. Eisenhower* (Lawrence, Kansas, 1979), p. 99; Eisenhower, *Waging Peace,* pp. 43, 667.
17. Lyon, *Eisenhower,* p. 699.
18. Cooper, *Lion's Last Roar,* pp. 157–58.
19. Kennett Love, *Suez: The Twice-Fought War* (New York, 1969), p. 503; Lyon, *Eisenhower,* p. 715.

20. Love, *Suez*, p. 504; Cooper, *Lion's Last Roar*, p. 171; Herman Finer, *Dulles Over Suez* (Chicago, 1964), p. 386; Emmet John Hughes, *The Ordeal of Power* (New York, 1963), pp. 217, 219.
21. Robert A. Divine, *Foreign Policy and U.S. Presidential Elections, 1952–1960* (New York, 1974), p. 169.
22. Love, *Suez*, pp. 614–15.
23. New York *Times*, November 7, 1956; Hughes, *Ordeal*, p. 223; Eisenhower, *Waging Peace*, p. 91.
24. *Ibid.*, p. 92.
25. Hoopes, *Dulles*, p. 362.
26. Sherman Adams, *Firsthand Report* (New York, 1961), pp. 259–70; Eden, *Full Circle*, p. 628; Lyon, *Eisenhower*, pp. 723–25; Engler, *Politics of Oil*, pp. 261–62.
27. Eisenhower, *Waging Peace*, pp. 178–79.
28. *Public Papers of the Presidents: Eisenhower, 1957*, pp. 7, 12–13.
29. Alexander L. George and Richard Smoke, *Deterrence in American Foreign Policy: Theory and Practice* (New York, 1974), pp. 326–27; Rowland Evans and Robert Novak, *Lyndon B. Johnson: The Exercise of Power* (New York, 1966), p. 190.
30. Eisenhower, *Waging Peace*, pp. 178, 182–83, 680.
31. Evans and Novak, *Johnson*, p. 191.
32. Cooper, *Lion's Last Roar*, pp. 249–50; Lyon, *Eisenhower*, p. 729; Evans and Novak, *Johnson*, p. 192.
33. Adams, *Firsthand Report*, pp. 280–85; Eisenhower, *Waging Peace*, pp. 186–87.
34. *Public Papers of the Presidents: Eisenhower, 1957*, pp. 147, 151–52, 154.
35. Cooper, *Lion's Last Roar*, pp. 252–53; Eisenhower, *Waging Peace*, pp. 189, 685.
36. Lyon, *Eisenhower*, p. 734.
37. Stookey, *America and the Arab States*, pp. 150–54.
38. Eisenhower, *Waging Peace*, pp. 265–68.
39. Mosley, *Power Play*, pp. 280–81.

40. Hoopes, *Dulles,* p. 435; Robert Cutler, *No Time for Rest* (Boston, 1966), pp. 363–64.

41. Eisenhower, *Waging Peace,* pp. 269–72; Robert Murphy, *Diplomat Among Warriors* (Garden City, N.Y., 1964), p. 398; Cutler, *No Time for Rest,* p. 364.

42. Murphy, *Diplomat,* p. 399; Eisenhower, *Waging Peace,* p. 275.

43. *Public Papers of the Presidents: Eisenhower, 1958,* pp. 549, 555; Barnet, *Intervention and Revolution,* pp. 148–49; George and Smoke, *Deterrence,* pp. 355–57.

44. Engler, *Politics of Oil,* p. 309; Eisenhower, *Waging Peace,* p. 278; Mosley, *Power Play,* p. 282.

45. Murphy, *Diplomat,* pp. 407–8; Stookey, *America and the Arab States,* pp. 155–56.

46. Eisenhower, *Waging Peace,* pp. 270, 274; Murphy, *Diplomat,* p. 398; Adams, *Firsthand Report,* p. 293.

47. Lyon, *Eisenhower,* p. 775. Lyon is confused by a typographical error in Eisenhower's memoirs that lists the number of American troops in Lebanon at 114,357. The correct number is 14,357, composed of 8,515 soldiers and 5,842 marines. *See* Eisenhower, *Waging Peace,* p. 286, and Arthur Larson, *The President Nobody Knew* (New York, 1968), p. 86.

CHAPTER 4: EISENHOWER AND THE RUSSIANS

1. Robert J. Donovan, *Eisenhower: The Inside Story* (New York, 1956), p. 41; Emmet John Hughes, *The Ordeal of Power* (New York, 1963), p. 101.

2. Townsend Hoopes, *The Devil and John Foster Dulles* (Boston, 1973), p. 170; Donovan, *Eisenhower,* p. 72.

3. Hughes, *Ordeal,* pp. 103–4.

4. Dwight D. Eisenhower, *Mandate for Change, 1953–1956*

(Garden City, N.Y., 1963), pp. 145–47; Hughes, *Ordeal*, p. 113.

5. Herbert S. Parmet, *Eisenhower and the American Crusades* (New York, 1972), pp. 279–80; James A. Nathan and James K. Oliver, *United States Foreign Policy and World Order* (Boston, 1976), p. 226; Eisenhower, *Mandate*, p. 148.

6. Coral Bell, *Negotiation from Strength* (New York, 1963), p. 106; Hoopes, *Dulles*, pp. 173–75.

7. Charles E. Bohlen, *Witness to History, 1929–1969* (New York, 1973), p. 371; Parmet, *Eisenhower*, pp. 281–82.

8. Donovan, *Eisenhower*, pp. 184–85; Lewis L. Strauss, *Men and Decisions* (Garden City, N.Y., 1962), p. 336.

9. Eisenhower, *Mandate*, p. 252; Donovan, *Eisenhower*, pp. 185–90; Sherman Adams, *Firsthand Report* (New York, 1961), p. 112.

10. Donovan, *Eisenhower*, pp. 190–97; Eisenhower, *Mandate*, pp. 253–54; Ralph Lapp, *The Weapons Culture* (Baltimore, 1969), pp. 119–20.

11. Peter Lyon, *Eisenhower: Portrait of the Hero* (Boston, 1974), p. 584; Eisenhower, *Mandate*, pp. 252, 254; Thomas F. Soapes, "A Cold Warrior Seeks Peace: Eisenhower's Strategy for Nuclear Disarmament," *Diplomatic History*, 4 (Winter 1980), p. 62.

12. Robert A. Divine, *Blowing on the Wind* (New York, 1978), pp. 3–13, 23–26.

13. Hoopes, *Dulles*, pp. 284–85; Bernhard G. Bechhoefer, *Postwar Negotiations for Arms Control* (Washington, 1961), p. 252; Lyon, *Eisenhower*, p. 627.

14. Elmo Richardson, *The Presidency of Dwight D. Eisenhower* (Lawrence, Kansas, 1979), p. 79.

15. Bechhoefer, *Postwar Negotiations*, p. 293.

16. Eisenhower, *Manadate*, p. 506; Adams, *Firsthand Report*, p. 177.

17. Donovan, *Eisenhower*, pp. 345–46; Hoopes, *Dulles*, p. 295; Eisenhower, *Mandate*, p. 515.

18. *Ibid.,* pp. 518, 519–20.
19. *Ibid.,* p. 520; Vernon A. Walters, *Silent Missions* (Garden City, N.Y., 1978), pp. 288–89.
20. Hoopes, *Dulles,* p. 297; Eisenhower, *Mandate,* p. 521; Bohlen, *Witness,* p. 384.
21. Lyon, *Eisenhower,* pp. 663–64; Parmet, *Eisenhower,* p. 406; Bechhoefer, *Postwar Negotiations,* pp. 256–57, 301–2; Soapes, "Cold Warrior Seeks Peace," pp. 65–66.
22. Hughes, *Ordeal,* p. 168; Harold Macmillan, *Tides of Fortune, 1945–1955* (New York, 1969), p. 624; Hoopes, *Dulles,* p. 301.
23. Donovan, *Eisenhower,* p. 350; Hoopes, *Dulles,* p. 297.
24. Divine, *Blowing on the Wind,* pp. 84–108, 113–38.
25. Eisenhower to Cole, May 27, 1957, Dwight D. Eisenhower Papers, Diary Series, Eisenhower Library, Abilene, Kansas; Divine, *Blowing on the Wind,* pp. 143–46.
26. Memorandum of conference with the President by Andrew J. Goodpaster, June 24, 1957, Eisenhower Papers, Diary Series; *Public Papers of the Presidents: Eisenhower, 1957,* pp. 498–99.
27. Memorandum of conference with the President by Andrew J. Goodpaster, March 24, 1958, Eisenhower Papers, Diary Series.
28. Divine, *Blowing on the Wind,* pp. 206–11.
29. Memorandum of conference with the President by Andrew J. Goodpaster, August 18, 1958, Eisenhower Papers, Diary Series.
30. Divine, *Blowing on the Wind,* pp. 225–40.
31. Jean Edward Smith, *The Defense of Berlin* (Baltimore, 1963), p. 178.
32. Ibid., pp. 159–62; Jack M. Schick, *The Berlin Crisis, 1958–1962* (Philadelphia, 1971), pp. 8–10; Bell, *Negotiation from Strength,* pp. 197–98; Charles C. Alexander, *Holding the Line: The Eisenhower Era, 1952–1961* (Bloomington, Ind., 1975), pp. 239–40.
33. Smith, *Defense of Berlin,* p. 154; Dwight D. Eisenhower,

Waging Peace, 1956–1961 (Garden City, N.Y., 1965), pp. 337–38; John S. D. Eisenhower, *Strictly Personal* (Garden City, N.Y., 1974), p. 216.

34. Douglas Kinnard, *President Eisenhower and Strategy Management* (Lexington, Kentucky, 1977), pp. 110–11; John Eisenhower, *Strictly Personal*, pp. 219–20; Eisenhower, *Waging Peace*, pp. 340–42.

35. Schick, *Berlin Crisis*, pp. 51–52.

36. Eisenhower, *Waging Peace*, pp. 354–55.

37. Richardson, *Presidency of Eisenhower*, pp. 160–61; Eisenhower, *Waging Peace*, pp. 432, 435; Lyon, *Eisenhower*, p. 800.

38. Schick, *Berlin Crisis*, pp. 100–104.

39. Eisenhower, *Waging Peace*, p. 449; Parmet, *Eisenhower*, p. 551.

40. Eisenhower, *Waging Peace*, p. 479; Divine, *Blowing on the Wind*, pp. 245–46, 254.

41. Harold Macmillan, *Riding the Storm, 1956–1959* (New York, 1971), pp. 647–48; Divine, *Blowing on the Wind*, pp. 255–61.

42. *Ibid.*, pp. 286, 295–98.

43. George B. Kistiakowsky, *A Scientist at the White House* (Cambridge, Mass., 1976), pp. 281–82; memorandum of conference with the President by Andrew J. Goodpaster, March 24, 1960, Eisenhower Papers, Diary Series.

44. Divine, *Blowing on the Wind*, pp. 301–2; Kistiakowsky, *Scientist*, p. 288; Harold Macmillan, *Pointing the Way, 1959–1961* (New York, 1972), pp. 188–91.

45. Smith, *Defense of Berlin*, pp. 216–21; Schick, *Berlin Crisis*, pp. 110–11.

46. James R. Killian, Jr., *Sputnik, Scientists and Eisenhower* (Cambridge, Mass., 1977), pp. 81–83; Parmet, *Eisenhower*, p. 528; Milton S. Eisenhower, *The President Is Calling* (Garden City, N.Y., 1974), p. 335; Bohlen, *Witness*, p. 466; Eisenhower, *Waging Peace*, pp. 544–49.

47. David Wise and Thomas B. Ross, *The U-2 Affair* (New

York, 1962), pp. 96–98, 130–31; John Eisenhower, *Strictly Personal*, p. 271; Alexander, *Holding the Line*, p. 265.

48. Eisenhower, *Waging Peace*, pp. 552–56; Lyon, *Eisenhower*, p. 811.

49. Kistiakowsky, *Scientist*, pp. 335–36; Eisenhower, *Waging Peace*, p. 558.

50. Kistiakowsky, *Scientist*, p. 375.

51. Richard M. Nixon, *Six Crises* (Garden City, New York., 1962), p. 161.

52. Hughes, *Ordeal of Power*, p. 349.

Index

Congress: told of National Security Council's role, 24; and policy in Indochina, 44; and Aswan Dam, 81; and Eisenhower Doctrine, 91–95; and Lebanon crisis, 99–100
Containment, doctrine of: modified by NSC, 34–35
Cuba, 155; and Castro, 152
Cutler, Robert, 100; as Special Assistant for National Security Affairs, 23–25; and Operation Wheaties, 112

Darlan, Jean, 8–9
Davis, A. C.: against Indochina intervention, 50
Decoupling, 141
Defense Department: and U-2 incident, 148
de Gaulle, Charles, 6, 9; and Berlin crisis, 133; and summit conference of 1960, 150
Democratic party: supports Eisenhower on Yalta, 26
Détente, 105–6
Deterrence: replaces containment, 39; in first Formosa Straits crisis, 61–66
Diem, Ngo Dinh: see Ngo Dinh Diem
Dien Bien Phu, 40, 42; surrenders, 47
Dillon, C. Douglas, 46; replies to Soviet threat, 147
Domino theory, 41–42
Donovan, Robert: on Eisenhower's image, 123
Dulles, Allen, 75, 87; on National Security Council, 24; on Suez crisis, 88
Dulles, John Foster, 25–26, 31,

117; and Republican foreign policy, 12; confers with Eisenhower on liberation and retaliation, 13–14; as secretary of state, 19–23; favors widening war in Korea, 28, 30; renews retaliation proposal, 34–35; and new doctrine of retaliation, 37–38; boosts Navarre Plan, 40; proposes united action to save Indochina, 43–45; warns Peking, 51; outlines new Indochina policy, 52–53; and SEATO, 53–54; and first Formosa Straits crisis, 56–58, 61–62, 64–65; and second Formosa Straits crisis, 67–68; and Suez crisis, 79–81; 83–85, 87, 98–99, 102–3; stricken with cancer, 87; and hard line toward Soviets, 106; and new Soviet line, 107; and summit proposal, 109; and Operation Wheaties, 112; and "open skies" concept, 118; and nuclear test ban, 125–29; and Berlin crisis, 133–34, 136; dies, 137; and Eisenhower's presidential style, 154
Dulles-Radford proposal, 35

Early, Steve: on Eisenhower's public relations, 8
East Germany: in Warsaw Pact, 117; and Berlin crisis, 131–32, 134–35, 138
Eden, Anthony: and Indochina settlement, 46–47; and Suez crisis, 81–82; upbraided by Eisenhower, 85; halts inva-

in Indochina, 39–41, 45–47;
record in Indochina, 42;
agrees to Geneva conference,
43; in SEATO, 54; and
seizure of Suez Canal, 81–82;
attacks Egypt, 84–88; leaves
Suez area, 90; and "open
skies," 120; and Berlin crisis,
133
Freedom programs: *see* Radio
Free Europe

Gallup poll: and "spirit of
Camp David," 139
Gaza Strip, 84, 89, 93, 95
Geneva: and Formosa talks, 64
Geneva Accords, 43, 54; U.S.
attitude toward, 52
Geneva Conferences: on arms
control, 118–23; on Berlin
crisis, 136–37; on nuclear test
ban, 140–46
Germany: rearmament of, 109,
116–17
GOP: *see* Republicans
Great Britain: and Korean policy, 21; in SEATO, 54; and
second Formosa crisis, 68, 69–
70; and Baghdad Pact, 79–80;
and Aswan Dam, 80; and
seizure of Suez Canal, 81–82;
attacks Egypt, 84–88; and
Western European Union,
117; and "open skies," 120;
and Berlin crisis, 133, 136–37
Gruenther, Alfred, 42–43, 122

Hagerty, James, 8, 53, 59, 63–64,
101
Hague Peace Conference, 20

HARDTACK: and test ban
issue, 127–29, 140–41
Herter, Christian: replaces
Dulles, 136; and Berlin crisis,
136–37; confirms U-2 espionage mission, 149–50
Hiroshima, 110
Ho Chi Minh, 39, 52
Honest John rockets, 100
Hoopes, Townsend, 83; praises
Eisenhower's Indochina policy, 54–55; on second Formosa crisis, 70
Hoover, Herbert, Jr.: arranges
oil settlement in Iran, 76–78
House of Representatives, Foreign Affairs Committee:
backs Eisenhower on Yalta,
26
Hughes, Emmet, 21, 29, 86–87;
writes "I shall go to Korea"
speech, 18; writes peace
speech, 107; on Geneva conference, 122; on Eisenhower's
style, 154
Humphrey, George: and massive
retaliation, 35–36
Hussein, King, 97
Hydrogen bomb: first tested,
110–11; Soviet test, 111

ICBM, 148
India, 29–30; not in SEATO, 54
Indochina: Communist insurgency in, 39; U.S. supports
French, 39–40; French strategy, 40; and Eisenhower's
policy assumptions, 41–44;
French record in, 42; Congress reluctant to intervene,
44–45; U.S. decides against
intervention, 47–50; U.S.

INDEX